THE AMERICAN KENNEL CLUB DOG CARE AND TRAINING

Second Edition

HOWELL
BOOK
HOUSE

Wiley Publishing, Inc.

Howell Book House

Published by Wiley Publishing, Inc., New York, NY

For general information on our other products and services, please contact our Customer Care Department within the U.S. at 800-762-2974, outside the U.S. at 317-572-3993 or fax 317-572-4002.

Wiley also publishes its books in a variety of electronic formats. Some content that appears in print may not be available in electronic books.

Library of Congress Cataloging-in-Publication Data is available from the publisher.

ISBN: 0-7645-3608-7
EAN: 9780764536083
UPC: 785555086197

Manufactured in the United States of America
5   4   3   2

Cover designed by Michael J. Freeland
Cover photograph by Winter/Churchill/DOGPHOTO.COM

CONTENTS

ACKNOWLEDGMENTS

Our goal in writing *The American Kennel Club Dog Care and Training,* **Second Edition,** was to provide the reader with a basic, general dog care and training book. This book offers general background information on topics such as considerations prior to adding a dog to your home, how you should go about selecting a puppy or older dog, and how you can register your dog with The American Kennel Club. Tips are provided on housebreaking, grooming, bathing, and health care. A new expanded chapter on training offers suggestions for teaching basic commands, and it describes for readers the many training activities available to owners and their dogs. Additional information regarding breeding, the background of The American Kennel Club, and first aid makes this a well-rounded, all-purpose book that should be on every dog owner's bookshelf.

Mary R. Burch, Ph.D., is The American Kennel Club's Canine Good Citizen Director. Dr. Burch is a member of the Dog Writer's Association of America and she is an award-winning dog writer. She is the author of *Volunteering with Your Pet, The Border Collie,* and *How Dogs Learn,* all published by Howell Book House. Dr. Burch is a Certified Applied Animal Behaviorist, and she has trained dogs to the advanced levels of obedience.

Dennis B. Sprung is the Vice President of Corporate Relations for The American Kennel Club. He was the project director for this extensive revision of *The AKC Dog Care and Training.* Involved in the sport of purebred dogs for over 30 years, Mr. Sprung has among other disciplines been an exhibitor, breeder, Judge, AKC Delegate, and Club President. He has traveled to dog shows worldwide and has interacted extensively with internationally recognized experts on a variety of canine topics.

We would like to acknowledge the following AKC staff members who reviewed and edited information relevant to their subject matter expertise:

Dolores Alonso	Patricia R. Krause	Ronald N. Rella
Mary Ann Alston	Marta Lewis	Wendy Serkin
Sharon Anderson	Michael Liosis	Tom Sharp
Noreen Baxter	Linda More	William Speck
Keith Frazier	Mari-Beth O'Neill	Maria Vazquez

Special thanks to Donald Schwartz, VMD for his contributions.

INTRODUCTION

For more than a century, The American Kennel Club has been a mainstay in the sport of purebred dogs. Today, it is among the world's best sources on the subject.

The AKC has produced *The American Kennel Club Dog Care and Training,* Second Edition, to supply you with information to use in getting started as a dog owner. The contents of this comprehensive book range from "how to select the best breed for you" to "registering your dog with The AKC."

A dog is a lifetime commitment, and this book provides important guidance in areas such as nutrition, grooming, and training. From these pages, you will learn to develop a healthy and mutually enjoyable long-term relationship with your newest family member.

A major benefit of AKC registration is the opportunity for you and your dog to participate in and enjoy a myriad of events. There is an activity for every dog and every owner, with competition levels for the newest novice, the most experienced veteran, and everyone in between. The AKC's Canine Good Citizen® Test demonstrates that your dog has mastered basic good manners A wide variety of competitive events are also available to you and your dog. AKC competitive events demonstrate teamwork and proficiency. These include dog shows, as well as Field Trials, Hunting Tests, Obedience, Agility, Tracking, Herding, Earthdog Tests, and Lure Coursing. Participation in these activities will enhance the bond between you and your canine companion, as well as lead to new friendships, years of enjoyment, and a lifetime of memories.

We hope that you will take advantage of the world of activity that AKC registration makes available to you and your dog. We look forward to seeing you soon at one of our many AKC events.

Alfred L. Cheauré
President/CEO

Alaskan Malamute. *Mary Bloom.*

The dog you share your life with reflects both what you expect from it and the care you devote to it. This is true for all dogs—stalwart sled dogs, playful children's companions, trusting puppies, and many more. It may take a little extra effort to find just the right dog for you, but the results will more than justify the search.

■ 1 ■

BEFORE YOU
GET A DOG

The time has come to get a dog. That's what your heart is calling for, and your head's not far behind. Before you know it, the car keys are tight in your hand and you hasten to find the nearest litter of puppies for sale.

Before you rush off, we urge you to slow down and *think!* Getting a dog represents a commitment that may last well over a decade. The decision to do so deserves careful consideration; without it, you may eventually wind up asking yourself how you could have done such a thing. Far too many dogs are abandoned because people are guilty of acting first and thinking later—too many people get a dog on impulse. We implore you not to join their ranks.

In the next few pages, we'll look into a number of factors that you should weigh carefully *before* you get a dog. This should save you, your family, and your dog the heartbreak of severing a disappointing relationship in the months to come. It will also help guide you toward getting the right dog at the start.

To do the right thing and make sure that you are a responsible dog owner, you'll need to think about several things before adding a dog to your family. You'll want to give a lot of thought as to whether or not this really is a good time for you to get a dog. This involves asking yourself why you want a dog. Once you decide that you are ready for a serious commitment in time, training, and love, and the time is right for adding a canine companion to your home, your homework begins. You'll need to make some important choices about the breed, size, activity level, and temperament of the dog you will get. You'll need to make some very practical decisions, such as, do you want a long or short-coated dog, as in, is vacuuming one of your least favorite activities? Let's look at the factors you'll need to take into consideration. Remember, being a responsible dog owner begins the moment you select your dog.

Think Why

Why do you want a dog? There are lots of good reasons to add a dog to your life, as well as some bad ones.

Keep in mind that if you're bringing a dog into your household, the relationship is not going to work unless *everyone* wants it to work—adults as well as kids. No matter how ardently the kids promise to care for the new dog, it's unrealistic to expect them to shoulder the full responsibility for the puppy's needs. Remember, when it's time to pay for food, shelter, and veterinary care, parents still foot the bills. Life will run a lot more smoothly if you want the dog as much as your kids.

Dogs deserve their popularity as pets for good reasons. They are adaptable. They are easily trained. Their lives are relatively long and healthy. But they are completely dependent on their owners. They must be fed a proper diet, and they need to see a veterinarian regularly, if for no other reason than to be vaccinated against major infectious diseases. Just like us, dogs get sick—and they age, not always gracefully. When they need people most, many owners find the responsibility too great. Please do not view dogs as disposable items, easy to cast out when the road turns bumpy. If you do, don't get a dog. Buy something without feelings, without the capacity to return your love. Dogs deserve better than that.

Bullmastiff. *Mary Bloom*   **Papillon.** *Mary Bloom*

Cavalier King Charles Spaniel. *Mary Bloom*

So *think* before you get a dog. Weigh all the facts carefully, select the right breed, and get ready to have your life enriched by the incomparable canine.

Think Size

All dogs start out small. And small is rarely a problem. But what about later, when puppyhood remains only a pleasant memory? You must be ready to meet the large dog's need for large space, plenty of food, and exercise, for starters. Many medium-size to large breeds are unsuitable for apartment life or any situation that limits their opportunity to work off energy. And these dogs *must* be obedience trained or problems are inevitable.

Where and how you live are important factors in considering the right size breed for you. City dwellers have different considerations than do rural residents. Many apartment complexes, while permitting dogs, limit their size. This limit is frequently determined by weight. And of course, if you're an especially finicky housekeeper, the larger the dog the larger the potential problems, even if it's just wet feet in the back hall on a rainy day.

American Eskimo Dogs. *Chet Jazierski*

Will you be traveling with your dog? Even a short trip with a big dog can become a crisis if you lack the appropriate vehicle to transport him or the physical strength to control him. As for vacationing with your pet, just try convincing hotel management that your 150-pound canine companion won't get one bit of dog hair in the hotel room. It can be tough.

Conversely, small dogs are ideal for some families, but may be endangered by others. Toy breeds are simply too delicate to compete with boisterous, out-of-control, young children. They need to live in a protected environment or they will not thrive.

Fortunately, it's easy to predict the adult height and weight of any purebred dog. Just find the American Kennel Club breed Standard for the breed you're interested in. The breed Standard describes the ideal specimen of the breed. It will give you a good idea of a typical adult's size. There are separate standards for all of the breeds recognized by The AKC. Remember, it is wise to view the parents of any puppy you're considering. Size is an inherited trait. In fact, one of the best reasons to buy a purebred puppy is that you have a much better chance of knowing what he will look like when he grows up. For now, we're talking about size, but several traits, from coat type to temperament, are also genetically determined.

So look beyond the enchanting puppy before you buy, and try to envision what a year's worth of growth will deliver: a perfect fit or potential problem?

Giant Schnauzers. *Mary Bloom*

Puppyhood is a very short period of a dog's life. When you select a breed, be sure that the adult animal is what you really want. When you think size, think about how much dog you can comfortably fit into your available space.

Think Purpose

By purpose, we mean the function for which the dog was originally bred. The diversity of our canine companions is wonderful and amazing. Some breeds were meant to be hunters, others guard dogs. In some parts of the world, dogs with great endurance brought livestock or produce to market or protected the farmer's animals. Several breeds were developed to retrieve, point, or flush game. Some followed a scent trail or ran down quarry. Still others found themselves pulling sleds and carts. Of course, some breeds were developed solely to offer pleasurable companionship to their owners. Knowing the dog's original purpose can be very important in determining what type of temperament will emerge in adulthood.

Let's return for a moment to the dog whose ancestors were bred to guard his owner's flock. All muscle, with a thick protective coat, this dog may paint a striking picture. But this type of dog may not be particularly sociable with people outside his own family. In fact, he may appear unapproachable. If you are looking for a breed that welcomes every man as its friend, life with this type of canine may prove disappointing. On the other hand, someone looking for a good watchdog might be thoroughly satisfied.

Field Spaniel. *Mary Bloom*   **Australian Cattle Dog.** *Mary Bloom*

The functions that various breeds were developed to perform are vitally important to their suitability as companions. Sporting dogs need not necessarily be used for hunting, but they are happy in an active role and enjoy outdoor pursuits. Herding dogs, in large part, have little or no access to livestock, but they are imprinted with the instincts and perceptions common to all stock dogs.

If you don't have lots of time to train a dog, you'll want to start out with a breed that has been bred to be easily trained. Some breeds learn commands with more ease than other breeds, and training them to respond to direction can be very gratifying. Describing some breeds as more trainable than others is not intended to be a criticism of any breed. It is a statement of fact that stems from recognizing the purposes for which different breeds were created.

The bottom line is, don't expect a dog whose ancestors have run like the wind for hundreds of generations to mature into a docile, sedentary animal. Such a breed would clearly not be the best choice, for example, for a retiree who wants a couch-mate rather than an active companion. AKC Customer Service receives frequent calls from owners who did not take the original purpose of the dog into account when selecting a breed: "I got this dog because I know he is smart, but he is driving me crazy in my apartment!" When we explain that a particular breed has been bred for centuries for a certain purpose, such as running for hours a day herding sheep or hunting birds, some owners are surprised to learn that the original purpose of the dog has any effect on the behavior of their dog.

So how do you avoid making this error? Go back to the breed Standard for a description of temperament for the average dog of this breed. Talk to people who already own or have owned a member of the breed. Contact the breed club for more information about the dog you're interested in. Visit a breeder with several dogs of this breed and spend some time with the dogs. Your research will pay off.

Think Care

The coat of a healthy dog can be eye-catching, from the glowing red jacket of an Irish Setter to the sculpted outline of a freshly groomed Kerry Blue Terrier or Bichon Frise. A beautiful dog with a beautiful coat is a pleasure to behold.

A dog's coat can also be a dog owner's nightmare. The picturesque coats commonly seen at dog shows are hardly the result of good intentions and benign neglect. We're talking about the creation of an art form, the result of long hours of preparation before each show and even more hours of maintenance in between. In real life, given ordinary constraints on time and energy, the image would probably be quite different.

Do you have sufficient time to bathe, groom, and care for the coat of a long-, fine-, or thick-haired dog? Do you comprehend what might happen if you ignore this job? If drastic measures like clipping the coat to near skin level don't bother you, great. If, on the other hand, the idea of damaging a distinctive coat goes against your grain, this is not the breed for you—unless you're prepared to spend a lot of time using brush and comb or having the dog professionally groomed.

Standard Poodle. *Mary Bloom*

If the idea of a heavy-coated dog appeals to you, be sure you are willing to provide the necessary upkeep to maintain the dog's appearance. A dog like this Standard Poodle would quickly become unsightly and offensive if her coat were neglected for any length of time.

Once again, check the breed Standards for a full description of the correct adult coat. Determine whether or not the breed that interests you has an undercoat. Many breeds grow thick undercoats that release piles of hair during ordinary shedding. Regular grooming helps contain the flood, but full-blown shedding can be problematic to the uninitiated. It can produce shell shock in a finicky homemaker, or it can mean another homeless dog. Find out about a breed's shedding characteristics and grooming needs before you bring the puppy home.

Another consideration is the potential monitoring of the condition of a dog's ears. Certain breeds have long, pendulous ears or lots of hair in the ear canals. You must remove any debris and hair frequently to prevent painful ear infections. Laziness on your part can result in agony to your dog, not to mention unnecessary veterinary bills. Are you prepared to assume this responsibility?

What about eyes? Lots of dogs never suffer from eye problems as long as they live. But dogs bred to have prominent eyes need time-consuming, special care to stay healthy. Again, these breeds would prove a poor choice for the person who wants a low-maintenance pet. These are just a few examples of the questions you must investigate and resolve before buying a dog.

Think Training

There is little doubt that the greatest single reason dogs are given up for adoption is the failure of their owners to train them adequately. Dogs are terrific companions, but keep in mind that they are still animals. Without proper training, the cutest puppy will grow up into a terror, either unmanageable, messy in the house, or both. A four-pound Pomeranian who forgets his manners on the Oriental rug is enough of a problem, but when the dog is a 65-pound Labrador Retriever, it's an absolute disaster. Realistically, you cannot live a happy life with such a dog.

Proper training means *someone* must be prepared to teach a dog what he can and cannot do. The good news is that training is relatively easy, if you are consistent and do it regularly from the day the dog arrives in your life. But you must be committed to doing a thorough and proper job of training right from the start, before problems get out of hand. And, there is the chance with any dog that you will need to be prepared to spend some time in training classes.

Think Cost

Purebred dogs aren't inexpensive. When the years of enjoyment you will have with your dog are considered, however, the purchase price should seem well spent. Even if you adopt a dog from the local shelter, there's *no such thing* as a free dog. "Free" lasts only until you get your first food and veterinary bill. In the beginning, there are periodic health checks, vaccinations, and dewormings. Your dog may need to start a heartworm preventative program.

As your dog matures, you will probably need to consider the cost of neutering your dog if he or she is not going to be part of a breeding program. Then, throughout the dog's life, there will be annual booster shots and visits to the veterinarian for this and that—some routine business, others due to unforeseen illness. All of these costs come out of your pocket, although pet insurance is now available and may be an option you wish to consider.

Pet insurance or no pet insurance, be prepared. In many parts of the country, veterinary costs are considerable.

In general, costs are lower for small dogs, since many surgical procedures, as well as hospitalization, are dependent upon the dog's weight (this goes for keeping your dog in a kennel, too). Medications and heartworm preventatives are also prescribed by weight, so they may be less expensive for smaller dogs. Smaller dogs also eat less than big dogs. If price is an issue, you may want to consider this right from the start.

If you're not prepared to groom your dog, you must also anticipate the cost of a professional groomer. Some dogs require grooming several times each year, so you may want to invest in the right equipment and learn to do it yourself, or be prepared to pay someone else to do the job. Better yet, if you don't want to invest the time or money in grooming a dog, consider a breed with minimal grooming requirements.

Think Use

Are you thinking about a show dog? Does home protection or perhaps a possible hunting partner spark your interest? Realistically, the overwhelming majority of dogs live their entire lives as companions, their first and foremost role being that of treasured pet. But if you are thinking about competing at dog shows or have any special need or use for a dog, now is the time to decide.

Borzoi. *Mary Bloom*   **Doberman Pinscher.** *Mary Bloom*

What do you plan to do with the dog you acquire? The vast majority of dogs spend their lives as pleasant household companions and no more. Pleasant companions can also make fine show dogs or satisfying field dogs. Many times, highly competitive animals spend the time between shows or trials just being dogs. You may want or need a dependable guard dog. If you do, remember that belligerent does not mean capable. A trustworthy guard dog with sound temperament and training does best.

The sport of showing dogs has huge appeal in the United States and is pursued by tens of thousands of avid enthusiasts. The sport for showing dogs is called "conformation dog shows." A lot can be said for the pleasures of raising a champion show dog. In fact, we'll investigate this engrossing topic in more detail later in this book. However, not every puppy, even those with champion parents, has show potential. If you think you might enjoy getting involved in the sport of showing dogs, make every effort to explore this possibility before you decide on a puppy, because it will affect what you buy.

Furthermore, have you considered whether you want a dog (male) or bitch (female)? And have you any thoughts about breeding dogs in the future? As far as which sex to buy, remember that bitches come into season ("heat") approximately twice each year, at which time they must be carefully isolated from other dogs to prevent pregnancy. The best birth control for a bitch is to have her spayed. Spaying (which makes a bitch ineligible for dog shows) has distinct health benefits as well. We'll look into spaying/neutering in more depth in a later chapter.

As for other variations between dogs and bitches (such as males being more aggressive, females more faithful, and so on), the truth is that a properly raised and trained canine makes a wonderful pet whether it is a male *or* a female.

Breeding is one activity you are best advised *not* to do. For certain, you're on the wrong track if you think breeding is a way to recoup the dog's purchase price (you won't come close, once the overall costs are tallied) or as a means of providing practical sex education for the kids. Breeding dogs as an activity should be restricted to well-educated, knowledgeable breeders who are experts in specific breeds.

Think Source

Unless you have already picked out your puppy, take a moment to think about where to purchase a well-bred, healthy dog.

An experienced breeder is your best bet for obtaining a high-quality animal. To begin with, breeders carefully select the parents of each litter to emphasize desirable attributes and minimize faults in their progeny. Breeders are committed to improving breed soundness—that is, physical and mental health—with every new generation.

Another good reason to buy a puppy from a breeder is that it gives you the opportunity to interact with the puppy's dam, littermates, and possibly the sire. You can, therefore, form a general impression of what the future holds for the puppy you take home.

Petit Basset Griffon Vendeen. *Mary Bloom*

The serious hobby breeder is the best source for your puppy. The breeder is motivated by a love of the breed and the desire to produce fine animals. Many times pet puppies come from the same litter as top winners, and the differences between them would not be apparent to most prospective owners.

Furthermore, buying from a breeder means that you're part of an extended family. Most breeders expect a call if the dog has a crisis at any stage in its life, so they can help you understand and cope with the problem. They seem to feel, in fact, that while their puppies must venture out into the world, they never really leave the fold. This can be especially comforting for first-time dog owners who can't even imagine what kinds of questions they'll have in the future. Come what may, the conscientious breeder will be there. Many responsible breeders will have contracts stating if for any reason in the lifetime of your dog you cannot keep it, they will take it back.

Responsible breeders will often be members of the national breed club for their breeds, they will have shown dogs in conformation shows, and their dogs will have championships. These breeders will be able to talk to you about the well-known kennels in the country for the breed and about the breed's history. Responsible breeders can tell you about genetic problems faced by the breed you are choosing, and will have a breeding plan designed to avoid specific genetic problems. Responsible breeders will have had their breeding stock tested for hip problems, eye problems, thyroid issues, and other disorders. This type of breeder is far different from the person who sells dogs via the local newspaper to anyone with a checkbook. These breeders are sometimes referred to as "backyard breeders." These individuals breed their pet-quality dogs simply to make extra money. "I'm looking for somebody in town who has a male (of this breed) I can breed my dog to," they say. Any dog will do, as long as it is of the same breed. At The AKC, we hear about the heartbreak when the owner has fallen in love with the new puppy and is calling us to say he has health problems requiring extensive medical care and the seller will do nothing to help.

Think Breed

For several important reasons, we think your new dog should be an AKC purebred. At the top of the list are matters of predictability and reliability.

In 2001, The American Kennel Club recognized over 150 breeds of dogs. Each of these breeds has been selectively bred and nurtured over time to consistently produce a dog with specific characteristics. Therefore, the purebred puppy you select today will grow up to be a typical member of his breed, with a distinct personality and appearance. This means that no surprises are lying in wait for you a year down the line; you should be rewarded with a dog that meets your expectations. Don't forget that getting a high-quality dog from a breeder is additional reassurance.

As for which breed to get, you alone know the needs of your family. Take your time and do a thorough investigation. To start, let's review the general characteristics of the breeds that make up the seven American Kennel Club Groups.

The AKC classifies each purebred as either a Sporting, Hound, Working, Terrier, Toy, Non-Sporting, or Herding dog. There is also a Miscellaneous Class for breeds seeking AKC acceptance; these are the breeds in the process of advancing from unrecognized to fully recognized in the eyes of The American Kennel Club. Dogs in the Miscellaneous Class may compete in obedience, agility, and tracking events, but not conformation dog shows. Breeds recently added to the Miscellaneous Class are Beaucerons, Black Russian Terriers, Glen of Imaal Terriers, Neapolitan Mastiffs, Nova Scotia Duck Tolling Retrievers, and Redbone Coonhounds.

Also related to registration is The AKC's Foundation Stock Service® (FSS). The FSS is an optional record-keeping service for purebred breeds not currently permitted to be registered with The AKC. The FSS allows rare-breed fanciers to work on improving their breeds while the records of the breed (including ownership records and stud books) are maintained in a secure and reliable manner.

Members of each of the seven Groups share, to some extent, a common bond, through breeding, purpose, or size. Let's look at a few generalizations about each Group that may guide you toward or drive you away from some canine contenders. A complete listing of all of the breeds in each group can be found on pages 22–23.

Sporting Dogs

Naturally active and alert, Sporting dogs make likeable, well-rounded companions. Members of this Group include pointers, retrievers, setters, and spaniels. Remarkable for their instincts in water and woods, many of these breeds actively continue to participate in hunting and other field activities. Potential owners of Sporting dogs need to realize that most of these dogs will require regular, invigorating exercise.

Sporting dogs are so popular, in fact, that several of the top-registered breeds in the United States are members of this Group. In the year 2001, occupying first and second positions of total AKC registrations were the Labrador Retriever and Golden Retriever, respectively. Together, these two breeds accounted for nearly 230,000 of the annual registrations recorded in The AKC's Stud Book.

Irish Setter. *Mary Bloom*

Setters make up just one of the families in the Sporting Group and have been known for centuries.

Hounds

Most hounds share the common ancestral trait of being used for hunting. Hounds, often classified as either sight hounds or scent hounds, rely on the senses of sight and smell for hunting. Some use acute scenting powers to follow a trail. Others demonstrate a phenomenal gift of stamina as they relentlessly run down quarry they've spotted at a distance. Beyond this, however, generalizations about hounds are hard to come by, since the Group encompasses quite a diverse lot. There are Pharaoh Hounds, Norwegian Elkhounds, Afghans, and Beagles, among others. Some hounds share the distinct ability to produce a unique sound known as baying. You might want to sample this sound before you decide to get a hound of your own.

Otterhound. *Mary Bloom*

The Hound Group includes some of the largest and smallest of breeds, as well as many of the most familiar and unusual. These dogs were developed to hunt large and small game. Divided into two categories, they hunted by sight or scent, and even today many are still used to do their breeds' work.

Pharaoh Hound. *Mary Bloom*

Dachshund. *The AKC*

Working Dogs

Dogs of the Working Group were bred to perform such jobs as guarding property, pulling sleds, and performing water rescues. They have been invaluable assets to humans throughout the ages. The Boxer, Siberian Husky, and Rottweiler are included in this Group, to name just a few. Quick to learn, these intelligent, capable animals make solid companions. Their considerable dimensions and strength alone, however, can make many working dogs unsuitable for average families. By virtue of their size alone, these dogs must be properly trained.

Great Pyrenees. *Mary Bloom*

The breeds in the Working Group include some of the best-loved dogs of all time. Many still serve humans in serious pursuits and demanding diversions as well.

Standard Schnauzer. *The AKC*

Terriers

People familiar with this Group invariably comment on the distinctive terrier personality. These are feisty, energetic dogs whose sizes range from fairly small, as in the Norfolk, Cairn, or West Highland White Terrier, to the grand Airedale Terrier. Terriers often have little tolerance for other animals, including other dogs. Their ancestors were bred to hunt and kill vermin. Many continue to project the attitude that they're always eager for a spirited argument.

Most terriers have wiry coats that require special care known as stripping in order to maintain a characteristic appearance. In general, they make engaging pets, but require owners with the determination to match their dogs' lively characteristics.

Miniature Bull Terrier. *Mary Bloom*

The terriers' distinctive personality is what often endears these breeds to dog lovers. These dogs are active, self-assured, and love to be wherever their favorite people are. By their nature, many terriers are diggers, and can be vocal. Therefore, if you think you'd like a terrier, be prepared for what these dogs truly are.

West Highland White Terrier. *Mary Bloom*

Japanese Chin. *Mary Bloom*

Toy dogs such as this Japanese Chin were developed solely for the pleasure they bring as pets. They are wonderful when space is limited but can make admirable pets in any setting.

Toy Dogs

The diminutive size and winsome expressions of Toy dogs illustrate the main function of this Group: to embody sheer delight. Don't let their tiny stature fool you, though—many Toys are tough as nails. Toy dogs will always be popular with city dwellers and people without much living space. The increasing popularity of Toy breeds over the past five years shows that more and more dog owners are discovering that Toys make ideal apartment dogs and terrific lap warmers on nippy nights.

Incidentally, small breeds may be found in every Group, not just the Toy Group. A future dog owner who wants to minimize some of the problems inherent in canines, such as shedding and cost of care, might want to consider a Toy breed. For people who have physical problems, training aside, it's easier to control a ten-pound dog than it is one that is ten times that size.

Non-Sporting Dogs

Non-Sporting dogs are also a diverse Group. Here we see sturdy animals with widely varying personalities and appearances that include the Chow Chow, Dalmatian, French Bulldog, and Keeshond. Talk about differences in size, coat, and visage! Some, like the Schipperke and Tibetan Spaniel, are uncommon sights in the average neighborhood. Others, however, like the Poodle and Lhasa Apso, have quite a large following. The history of each of the Non-Sporting breeds is fascinating. If you're considering a Non-Sporting breed, take a look at the job the dog was bred to do. The job descriptions of this Group are as varied as their appearances! The Non-Sporting Group has dogs who were used on boats, dogs who were used as guard dogs, and dogs who were used for sporting and a variety of other purposes.

Schipperke. *Mary Bloom*

Dalmatian. *Mary Bloom*

The breeds in the Non-Sporting Group are a varied collection in terms of size, coat, personality, and overall appearance. Some Non-Sporting breeds are seldom encountered outside a dog show, while others are universal favorites.

Herding Dogs

The seventh and final Group embraces the Herding dogs. The Herding Group, created in 1983, is also the newest AKC classification; most of its members were formerly members of the Working Group. All 18 breeds (German Shepherd Dog, Collie, and Old English Sheepdog among them) share the fabulous ability to control the movement of other animals. A remarkable example is the low-set Corgi, perhaps one foot tall at the shoulders, who can drive a herd of cows many times its size to pasture by leaping and nipping at the cows' heels. The vast majority of Herding dogs, as household pets, never cross paths with a farm animal. Nevertheless, pure instinct prompts many of these dogs to gently herd their owners, especially the children of the family. In general, these intelligent dogs make excellent companions and respond beautifully to training exercises.

Pembroke Welsh Corgi. *Mary Bloom*   Briard. *Mary Bloom*

The breeds in the Herding Group enabled humans to change from hunter to farmer and in so doing helped advance civilization. The variety among the Herding breeds reflects the conditions in which the dogs were developed and the needs of their environments. Today, Herding dogs are regarded among the most desirable and intelligent of breeds.

AKC Registered Breeds

The American Kennel Club *Complete Dog Book* is the perfect place to find information on each breed. This volume contains pictures, histories, and official breed Standards for all AKC-recognized breeds. You can also learn more about specific breeds on The AKC's website, www.akc.org.

Here is a complete list of the more than 150 breeds recognized by The AKC. The listing is by Group, with members arranged in alphabetical order. Traditionally, the Groups are assigned numerical designations of one (I) to seven (VII), with the Sporting being I, Hounds II, Working III, Terrier IV, Toy V, Non-Sporting VI, and Herding VII. You'll need this information if you go to a dog show in order to figure out who's being judged when and where.

BREEDS CURRENTLY RECOGNIZED BY THE AMERICAN KENNEL CLUB

I SPORTING GROUP

Brittany
Pointer
German Shorthaired Pointer
German Wirehaired Pointer
Chesapeake Bay Retriever
Curly-Coated Retriever
Flat-Coated Retriever
Golden Retriever
Labrador Retriever
English Setter
Gordon Setter
Irish Setter
American Water Spaniel
Clumber Spaniel
Cocker Spaniel
English Cocker Spaniel
English Springer Spaniel
Field Spaniel
Irish Water Spaniel
Sussex Spaniel
Welsh Springer Spaniel
Spinone Italiano
Vizslas
Weimaraner
Wirehaired Pointing Griffon

II HOUND GROUP

Afghan Hound
Basenji
Basset Hound
Beagle

Black & Tan Coonhound
Bloodhound
Borzoi
Dachshund
American Foxhound
English Foxhound
Greyhound
Harrier
Ibizan Hound
Irish Wolfhound
Norwegian Elkhound
Otterhound
Petit Basset Griffon Vendeen
Pharaoh Hound
Rhodesian Ridgeback
Saluki
Scottish Deerhound
Whippet

III WORKING GROUP

Akita
Alaskan Malamute
Anatolian Shepherd
Bernese Mountain Dog
Boxer
Bullmastiff
Doberman Pinscher
Giant Schnauzer
Great Dane
Great Pyrenees
Greater Swiss Mountain Dog
Komondor

Kuvasz
Mastiff
Newfoundland
Portuguese Water Dog
Rottweiler
Saint Bernard
Samoyed
Siberian Husky
Standard Schnauzer

IV TERRIER GROUP

Airedale Terrier
American Staffordshire Terrier
Australian Terrier
Bedlington Terrier
Border Terrier
Bull Terrier
Cairn Terrier
Dandie Dinmont Terrier
Smooth Fox Terrier
Wire Fox Terrier
Irish Terrier
Jack Russell Terrier
Kerry Blue Terrier
Lakeland Terrier
Standard Manchester Terrier
Miniature Bull Terrier
Miniature Schnauzer
Norfolk Terrier
Norwich Terrier
Scottish Terrier
Sealyham Terrier

Skye Terrier
Soft Coated Wheaten Terrier
Staffordshire Bull Terrier
Welsh Terrier
West Highland White Terrier

V TOY GROUP

Affenpinscher
Brussels Griffon
Cavalier King Charles Spaniel
Chihuahua
Chinese Crested
English Toy Spaniel
Havanese
Italian Greyhound
Japanese Chin
Maltese
Toy Manchester Terrier
Miniature Pinscher
Papillon
Pekingese
Pomeranian
Toy Poodle
Pug
Shih Tzu
Silky Terrier
Yorkshire Terrier

VI NON-SPORTING GROUP

American Eskimo Dog
Bichon Frise
Boston Terrier
Bulldog
Chinese Shar-Pei
Chow Chow
Dalmatian
Finnish Spitz
French Bulldog
Keeshond
Lhasa Apso
Lowchen
Poodle
Schipperke
Shiba Inu
Tibetan Spaniel
Tibetan Terrier

VII HERDING GROUP

Australian Cattle Dog
Australian Shepherd
Bearded Collie
Belgian Malinois
Belgian Sheepdog

Belgian Tervuren
Border Collie
Bouvier des flandres
Briard
Canaan Dog
Collie
German Shepherd Dog
Old English Sheepdog
Polish Lowland Sheepdog
Pulik
Shetland Sheepdog
Cardigan Welsh Corgi
Pembroke Welsh Corgi

MISCELLANEOUS GROUP

Beauceron
Black Russian Terrier
German Pinscher
Glen of Imaal Terrier
Neopolitan Mastiff
Nova Scotia Duck Tolling
  Retriever
Plott Hound
Redbone Coonhound
Toy Fox Terrier

West Highland White Terriers. *Chet Jezierski*

■ 2 ■

SELECTING AND REGISTERING YOUR PUPPY

It's probably apparent by now that choosing the right dog is not a simple task and should not be made impulsively. The job is well worth the effort, however. Consider it an investment intended to save you, your family, and the animal a lot of potential grief.

Now that your thoughts are better attuned to your individual needs and desires in a dog, it's time to contact some valuable resources and enhance your breed knowledge.

These resources include breeders, veterinarians, dog-show people, friends, The AKC, and even neighbors. You'd be surprised by the kinds of experiences people have had with dogs over the years. Breeders, certainly, are very knowledgeable and eager to discuss the virtues of their breed with newcomers. They also offer you an excellent opportunity to see real dogs in real settings. You can find responsible breeders through contacts found in the section named Breeds on The AKC's website at www.akc.org.

Don't hesitate to tell breeders what you want in a dog so they can offer an educated opinion about whether their breed is right for you. Finding breeders is as easy as looking in the classified section of newspapers or dog magazines, asking someone who already owns a dog, or contacting The American Kennel Club.

Also, there are numerous publications written specifically about each breed. You can find these publications online, or you can browse through them at your local library or bookstore. A representative of the breed club, which is organized by people who share a common interest in one breed of dog, can provide you with good references. The American Kennel Club has an up-to-date list of breed clubs and will help direct you to the nearest breed club representative. If you don't have access to The AKC's website, you can call The American Kennel Club's Customer Service line at 919-233-9767 for help.

As far as seeing the real thing, however, especially when you're comparing breeds, there's nothing like attending a dog show. Dog shows provide the opportunity to see a parade of fine specimens of each breed, and you might better appreciate whether a particular breed is right for you. Seen up close, the breed that looked perfect in a photograph may suddenly make you wonder whether the kids will be walking the dog or the other way around.

Most probably you will find exactly what you've been looking for. Try to engage people around the show ring in some conversation. Keep in mind that the ring participants are preoccupied with their work, so talk to handlers or owners once their time in the limelight is over. These are great ways of getting to know a breed.

Selecting the Puppy

Puppies are normally mature enough to leave their mother and littermates when they are eight weeks old. Under no circumstances should you bring home a puppy less than eight weeks of age. It's important to know that the puppy is strong enough to be on her own.

The puppy you select should appear bright, inquisitive, and alert—in other words, healthy. No matter what your heart says, do not select a puppy who seems ill or weak, or has a runny nose, watery eyes, or apparent fever. The coat should appear bright and shining, and the puppy should be of a good weight, never thin or excessively potbellied. You should avoid a trembling, shy puppy or one who seems snappy and bad tempered. Don't buy a puppy from a litter in which disease seems to be present.

Chesapeake Bay Retriever. *Beth Hanson*

Saint Bernard. *Chet Jezierski*

It is imperative to seek a veterinarian's opinion on the puppy's health as soon as possible after you bring the puppy home. Bring along any documentation provided by the seller that states dates of vaccination, parasite treatment, or history of illness. After a veterinarian has assured you that everything seems to be all right, your life with your new puppy has begun.

AKC Registration

Before we get much further, let's take a few moments to clarify The AKC's involvement in the buying or selling of dogs. In point of fact, *it does neither.* The AKC is, primarily, an organization that registers over one million purebred dogs annually and governs the sport of dogs in the United States. Over 15,000 different sporting events, from dog shows to Obedience to Performance Events, are held under The AKC's rules and regulations each year.

There are no individual "members" in The American Kennel Club. The AKC is a "club of clubs," founded in 1884 by show-giving clubs to bring order to the sport of dogs. One of the oldest sport-governing bodies in the United States, The AKC continues to champion the cause of purebred dogs through events that reward breed soundness and ability as well as through public education.

American Eskimo Dog. *Chet Jezierski*

Even if you have never had a dog before, there are certain things you can recognize when you set out to select a puppy. A well-socialized puppy with good temperament is often a reflection of its parents. Try to observe the mother for a clue to this important aspect. The puppy you consider should give every indication of good health and vitality, and should be outgoing. Also observe the puppies as they play together. This gives you a good idea of the dominant and submissive members of a litter and gives you a better chance of finding the right puppy for you.

Your relationship with The AKC begins as you complete the purchase of your purebred puppy or dog. When you buy a dog that is represented as being eligible for registration with The American Kennel Club, you should receive an AKC application form properly filled out by the seller. Once you complete the application and submit it to The AKC with the proper fee, if all is in order, the dog will be registered in your name and The AKC will mail out your official registration certificate.

If the dog has already been registered by the previous owner, the seller should furnish you with the dog's registration certificate. The owner should complete the reverse side of the certificate to indicate transfer to you.

If the seller does not have the AKC registration application or registration certificate available at the time you acquire the dog, the seller should give you a written bill of sale that includes the following information:

- breed, sex, color, and markings of the dog
- date of birth of the dog
- registered names and numbers of the dog's sire and dam
- litter number (when available)
- name and address of the breeder
- date sold or delivered

The bill of sale should also indicate when you might expect to receive the actual AKC registration papers. Anyone acquiring a dog represented as being eligible for AKC registration should realize that it is his responsibility to obtain complete identification of the dog as described above. If the seller is unable or unwilling to provide either proper AKC

AKC DOG REGISTRATION APPLICATION
** This form is **NOT** a certificate of registration. **
APPLICATION ISSUE DATE:MAY 10 2001

DO NOT WRITE IN SPACE ABOVE

BREED	CHINESE SHAR-PEI
DATE OF BIRTH	MARCH 18 2001
SIRE	CH SAMPLE GONNA WIN T'DAY NM777777/02 (4-99)
DAM	CH SAMPLE REALLY TRY HARDER CD NM000000/01 (12-98)
BREEDER	JILL SAMPLE
LITTER OWNER	JILL SAMPLE 123 SAMPLE STREET SAMPLE, SA 88888-8888

LITTER NUMBER NM999999/01

LITTER OWNER COMPLETES BLUE SECTIONS-NEW OWNER COMPLETES RED SECTIONS   DIRECTIONS:

STEP 1. CHECK YOUR REGISTRATION OPTION:

OPTION 1 ☐ $40.00
*Dog Care and Training Video
*Three Generation AKC Certified Pedigree
(traces back three generations
of your dog's ancestry)
*AKC Registration

OPTION 2 ☐ $32.00
*Three Generation AKC Certified Pedigree
(traces back three generations
of your dog's ancestry)
*AKC Registration

OPTION 3 ☐ $15.00
*AKC Registration only

PLEASE NOTE: ALL ITEMS ARE MAILED SEPARATELY

STEP 1. Check a registration option. See credit card payment information below.

Please pay by check, money order or credit card (see below).   DO NOT SEND CASH
For applications received more than one year after issue date, add $35.00.
For applications received more than two years after issue date, add $65.00 and include explanation for late registration.

☐ VISA ☐ Amex ☐ MasterCard

NUMBER   EXP DATE   SIGNATURE

Late fees will be added to credit card charges. Supplemental transfers $15.00 each.

STEP 2. NAME OF DOG:

THE PERSON WHO OWNS THE DOG AT THE TIME THIS APPLICATION IS SUBMITTED HAS THE RIGHT TO NAME IT.

STEP 2. PRINT one letter per space. Skip a space between words. Choose a unique name. Do not use numbers. Names are subject to AKC approval. Once a dog is registered, its name cannot be changed.

STEP 3. I HEREBY GIVE MY PERMISSION TO USE MY REGISTERED KENNEL NAME:

SIGNATURE OF KENNEL NAME OWNER   REGISTERED KENNEL NAME   CUSTOMER #

STEP 3. If an AKC registered kennel name is being used as a part of this dog's name, the owner of the registered kennel name **MUST** sign here.

STEP 4. CHECK SEX OF DOG YOU ARE REGISTERING:

☐ MALE   ☐ FEMALE

STEP 4. Check sex of this dog.

STEP 5. CHECK COLOR AND MARKINGS:

COLOR:
☐ 002 APRICOT
☐ 037 BLUE
☐ 076 CREAM
☐ 140 RED

☐ 007 BLACK
☐ 071 CHOCOLATE
☐ 082 FAWN
☐ 164 SABLE

MARKINGS:
☐ 042 DILUTE

STEP 5. Check the color and/or marking pattern that most closely describes the dog.

M00F01   ➤ PLEASE COMPLETE REVERSE SIDE FOR BALANCE OF APPLICATION ◄
© 1999 The American Kennel Club Inc.

The individual registration application covers the transfer of ownership from a puppy's breeder to its new owner. (Page 1 of 2.)

papers or a signed bill of sale with complete identifying information, *do not buy the dog!*

If you have complete breeding information but are experiencing difficulty obtaining registration papers, contact The AKC. Send along copies of your bill of sale or the identifying information you received at the time of purchase, the complete name and address of the person from whom you acquired the dog, and an explanation of what efforts you have made to obtain the papers. Send the information to: The American Kennel Club, 5580 Centerview Drive, Raleigh, NC 27606.

STEP 6. CHECK REGISTRATION TYPE:

☐ FULL   ☐ LIMITED

If no box is checked, dog will be given full registration.
Any correction must be accompanied by a written explanation from the litter owner.

STEP 6. Full: May be used as registrable breeding stock. Entry in dog events unrestricted. **LIMITED:** **Not** to be used for breeding stock. Entry in dog events is restricted.

STEP 7. CHECK OWNERSHIP AND FILL IN TRANSFER DATE:

☐ I (we) still own this dog and apply for registration and to have ownership recorded in my (our) name(s). Go to step 10.

☐ I (we) transferred this dog DIRECTLY to the NEW OWNER(S) on this date.

MONTH / DAY / YEAR

STEP 7. Check one box. **Enter the date that new owners took possession of the dog.** If the dog is to be registered in the name of the litter owner(s), skip steps 8 & 9.

STEP 8. PRINT NAME(S) OF NEW OWNER/CO-OWNER: I (we) apply to The American Kennel Club to have a registration certificate for this dog issued in my (our) name(s), and certify that I (we) acquired this dog on the date stated **directly** from the owner(s) of the litter. I (we) agree to abide by all American Kennel Club rules and regulations. I (we) understand that if the limited box in Step 6 has been checked by the litter owner(s), I (we) will receive a limited registration certificate.

STEP 8. Litter owner must print names as they will appear on Registration certificate and as recorded by litter owner. Print one name per line unless there are more than two co-owners.

1. NEW OWNER NAME   PLEASE PRINT

2. ADDRESS

3. CITY   STATE ☐☐   ZIP ☐☐☐☐☐ – ☐☐☐☐

4. E-MAIL ADDRESS   PHONE ☐☐☐ – ☐☐☐ – ☐☐☐☐

1. NEW CO-OWNER NAME   PLEASE PRINT

2. ADDRESS

3. CITY   STATE ☐☐   ZIP ☐☐☐☐☐ – ☐☐☐☐

4. E-MAIL ADDRESS   PHONE ☐☐☐ – ☐☐☐ – ☐☐☐☐

STEP 9. NEW OWNER(S) READ AND SIGN:

NEW OWNER SIGNATURE   NEW OWNER PLEASE SIGN

NEW CO-OWNER(S) SIGNATURE(S)   NEW CO-OWNER PLEASE SIGN

STEP 9. Each New Owner and Co-owner must sign separately.

IF THE NEW OWNERS LISTED ABOVE HAVE TRANSFERRED THIS DOG TO SOME OTHER PERSON(S), A *SUPPLEMENTAL TRANSFER STATEMENT* (Form# AXTRND) AND $15.00 FEE MUST ACCOMPANY THIS APPLICATION FOR EACH INTERMEDIATE TRANSFER. THESE FORMS ARE AVAILABLE FROM THE AMERICAN KENNEL CLUB AT THE ADDRESS SHOWN BELOW.

STEP 10. LITTER OWNER(S) READ AND SIGN: "I certify by my signature that all the information appearing on this application is correct, and that I am in good standing with The American Kennel Club."

STEP 10. ALL individuals whose names appear to the left MUST sign in the space indicated.

SIGNATURE OF JILL SAMPLE   DATE

NM999999/01

Corrections may cause a delay of registration for explanations. The AKC reserves the right to revoke for cause any registration certificate issued. A misrepresentation on this application is cause for cancellation and may result in loss of all AKC privileges for those individuals who violate the integrity of this application. All submitted applications become the property of the AKC.

If you need assistance filling out this application, additional forms or information, call AKC customer service (919) 233-9767   8:30 AM-5:00 PM Eastern Time Monday through Friday.

Please send completed form with appropriate fees to: **American Kennel Club**
PO Box 37902
Or Fax both sides of this form to: (919) 233-3627   **Raleigh, NC 27627-7902**

PLEASE NOTE: Applications take approximately three weeks to process. Please wait before calling AKC to check on the status of your application until after that time period has elapsed.

3   ADREG2 (8/01)

Page 2 of the individual registration application.

You can also find information about the registration process at The AKC's website.

Limited Registration

The AKC also provides the option for registering dogs with a limited registration. This option permits breeders to register dogs as "not for breeding purposes." This means that in the opinion of the breeder, the puppy demonstrates a trait or fault that the breeder does not wish to perpetuate. This is for the good of the breed. This fault may be as minor as an unaligned tooth or poor tail placement. This puppy can be a wonderful pet for someone, but is not of breeding caliber.

Dogs with limited registration are likely to otherwise make outstanding pets. The price for the limited registration puppy will probably be considerably less than for a littermate who does not have characteristics of concern to the breeder. A dog with limited registration is eligible to compete in all AKC-licensed events except breed competition at an AKC-licensed dog show.

"AKC Reg." Kennels—What Does It Mean?

Many people want to know the significance of "AKC Reg." when it appears after the name of a kennel. This simply means that the kennel's name is protected for the sole use of its owner in *naming* dogs to be registered. It does not imply a specific stamp of approval by The AKC.

The American Kennel Club and Quality

The serious breeders and exhibitors who founded The American Kennel Club as an organization to protect and promote purebred dogs have been successful beyond their wildest dreams. Not only have purebred dogs emerged as the beloved companions of millions of Americans, but the very identification of dogs as "AKC registered" has become synonymous with "quality" in the eyes of the public.

This has come about for good reason. The serious dog fancy in this country has bred outstanding dogs—with stable temperaments, healthy bodies, and good looks. Today's dogs are the result of untold years of devoted work by breeders to concentrate the best in their breed. They've carefully scrutinized each sire and dam before using them to perpetuate their kind, and then provided mother and offspring with the absolute best care possible for a good start in life.

Take advantage of the sweat and tears responsible breeders have poured into their work, and when it is time to get a dog, buy a high-quality puppy *from a responsible breeder.* They're not difficult to find. If you think that buying puppies from breeders means dealing with highfalutin people, you're in for a surprise. You're also going to be surprised if you think that the price of a pet puppy from a serious breeder will be too high. Actually, you can expect to pay no more, and in many cases less, for a puppy from a serious breeder than from a typical retail source of supply.

So please think long and hard about getting a dog. Then think again. The effort you put into deciding what breed is right for you and then obtaining the dog from the best possible source will reward you many times over during your dog's lifetime.

Dachshunds. *Beth Hanson*

While being separated from mother and siblings is traumatic for many puppies, they soon learn that they don't need to share their new people with any other dogs. Best of all, the adjustment period is usually very brief.

▪ 3 ▪

PUPPY CARE BASICS

Not surprisingly, your new puppy may seem a little lonely for the first few days. Try looking at circumstances from her point of view: One moment she's lying around with her mother, brothers, and sisters, romping and napping and feeling secure in the crowd. Suddenly, the scene is unfamiliar, and she's all *alone*. Who wouldn't be a little shaken up?

But soon your puppy will start to recognize *you* as "family" and learn that your home is her source of comfort and happiness. The bond between you will begin to form and grow before you know it. So hang in there for the first few nights when you hear signs of distress and lend support from the heart, which is easy, and the head, which may require some adjustment on your part.

When it comes to raising your puppy, your head isn't the only thing that may need some adjustment. You might need to adjust your whole lifestyle until you get this young animal trained and adapted to living in your family.

There is no doubt about it. Raising a puppy is incredibly hard work. But if you invest the time and energy and do it right, you'll have one of the most joyous experiences in your whole life. When you are the owner of a well-adjusted older dog, you'll look back and think that the puppy time was far too short. Photography buffs can take hundreds of pictures of puppies as they grow up and still think they should have taken more photos before the puppy days passed into memory. There's nothing like a sweet puppy falling asleep in your arms or following you everywhere you go.

Remember, the puppy you are raising today will be the dog you will have as a companion tomorrow. A good start in life will make all the difference in shaping a devoted, trusting companion.

To help your puppy get a good start in your household, you'll need to address several major issues. These are play time, adequate exercise, sleeping arrangements, housetraining (including crate training or paper training), feeding, bathing and grooming, and toothbrushing. You'll eventually need to make some decisions about spaying or neutering your dog. In some cases, you might need to deal with minor health problems. For these and more serious problems, you'll want a veterinarian you can trust. You'll need to choose the right veterinarian for you as one step in preparing for puppy raising.

Puppy Play Time

Puppies come into this world full of energy, looking for new adventures. Seeing the world through innocent puppy eyes is a gift that you will thoroughly enjoy and reminisce about when it is over. Structured play time is an important activity for puppies. Play time stimulates intellectual growth and gives you a chance to teach your puppy how to interact with you. If you want to maximize your pup's learning and the bonding experience, set aside some time for play every day.

"Puppy play time" is a time devoted to bonding with your puppy through games she will find intriguing, stimulating and completely rewarding. You will need some comfortable clothes, a variety of toys, and about 10 to 15 minutes of very relaxed time.

If you had the chance to observe your puppy with her littermates before you brought her home, you no doubt noticed the rough-and-tumble fun the puppies had as they played with each other. Your goal is to continue this stimulating, interesting, highly tactile experience as much as possible.

You'll need to get some toys for your play sessions with your puppy. Small soft toys, rope toys, tennis balls, and other items now are available in abundance, depending on the age and size of your puppy. Remember that puppies like to chew, so some toys may need to be used only when you are present to supervise.

With the ball, you can teach beginning retrieves, and with the soft toys you can play hide-and-seek. Each "game" can last for 30 to 90 seconds before your puppy gets bored; then you will need to move on to another one. Your puppy will be delighted day after day to see you pull out the toys, find your favorite spot on the floor, and call his name to "let the games begin."

Puppy play time will teach you a lot about your puppy's development, interests, and instincts. As your puppy matures, the games will change, and you will find new, more age-appropriate toys to capture his interests.

As your puppy begins to appreciate the time you spend together, you'll begin thinking of play time as the reward you've earned for all of your puppy-raising efforts. Soon you will discover that you look forward to your special time with your puppy each day as much as he does.

Adequate Exercise

All puppies need exercise in order to grow and develop properly. Exercise helps muscles grow strong and helps puppies develop coordination and balance. In addition to the physical benefits of exercise, there are other benefits.

If you brought your puppy home when she was very young, there is a good chance you are working on housetraining her. Providing adequate exercise helps keep your puppy's eliminations on a regular schedule. Exercise can stimulate your puppy's bowels and bladder, so regularly scheduled exercise can actually aid with the housetraining process.

Exercise also helps with your puppy's behavior. Puppies who receive adequate exercise are less likely to find activities for themselves and get into trouble.

It is important that you don't get carried away and give your puppy too much exercise. Check with your veterinarian if you have questions about the amount and types of exercise that are appropriate for your dog.

Sleeping Arrangements

You'll need to make some decisions about your puppy's sleeping arrangements. Some owners prefer that their dogs sleep in a crate. Crates for nighttime sleeping can be especially useful when dogs are not yet housetrained.

Once your dog is housetrained and has learned some basic good manners, you might decide she has earned the right to sleep uncrated in the bedroom or some other room of the house. There are many types of commercial dog beds available if you want to provide a comfy bed for your dog. You can teach your dog the command, "Get in your bed."

Whatever you decide about where your dog will sleep, remember to give her a chance to relieve herself one more time before you go to bed at night and get her outside as soon as possible in the morning.

Housetraining Your Dog

Dogs are not good companions unless they are completely house-trained—no "accidents," not even an occasional one. Otherwise, you can't trust them inside your home for fear they'll do the unthinkable, and repeated episodes of this kind will surely strain your relationship.

In fact, armies of dogs are abandoned each year by people who claim their dogs are incapable of being housetrained. This is a fallacy. All dogs can be housetrained, if their owners are consistent, as well as persistent, in training them. Some breeds need more time to learn the lesson than other breeds, but no normal dog is a hopeless case.

Be fair. Don't expect a puppy to train herself and don't expect total control overnight. Just select a method of housebreaking and follow it to the letter until the job is done. There will be training lapses in the beginning, probably just about when you think you're home free. This is only natural, and just means that you'll have to retreat a little and refresh the dog's memory. Once the message is instilled, however, it should take the most extreme of circumstances (like being ill) to make your dog violate her training.

Golden Retriever. *Diane Vasey*

There are two basic housebreaking techniques: crate training and paper training. Crate training is preferred, because it teaches direct housekeeping: That is, the single appropriate place to be used for elimination is the great outdoors. Paper training, unless you want your dog to keep eliminating in a designated location inside your home, should be viewed as an intermediate step toward teaching control until the dog is taken out. You may need to employ paper training because of treacherous weather conditions or some other special circumstance, such as being advised not to expose the puppy to the outdoors until inoculations have given her adequate immunity against disease. On the other hand, some apartment dwellers with small dogs are content to live with a paper-trained animal on a permanent basis for the sake of convenience.

Crate Training

Crate training is simple. Basically, it involves taking your puppy outside frequently, and praising him when he relieves himself. During the crate-training process, your puppy will spend her time inside either confined to a large, sleeping/living box (the crate) or under carefully supervised liberty. At night or when you're about to leave for a few hours, take the puppy outside to relieve herself, and then place her back in the crate. When you get up in the morning or arrive home, immediately take the puppy outside again, and then give her freedom to play in a confined area under your watchful eye.

Some experts in animal behavior believe that puppies adapt readily to crate training because their wild ancestors were den animals, and the crate becomes your puppy's personal den. Thus, crate training proceeds on the simple principle that dogs, as naturally clean animals, will do what they can to avoid soiling their den space. By confining a puppy to her crate at certain times of the day and night, she learns to control the urge to empty her bladder or bowels until she's allowed outside, whereupon she is rewarded through praise for a job well done.

If errors happen, and they will from time to time during the training period, immediately take the puppy outside to an area she has used previously, to remind her about the only permissible place to go. Remember to be fair. A young puppy needs to eliminate often, so take her out as often as you can in the early days before she has developed a measure of control. Puppies must be taken out about an hour after each feeding. Gradually, with age, your puppy will be able to contain herself for longer periods, and then you can reduce the required outings to approximately four daily.

Norfolk Terrier. *Chet Jezierski*

Provided your puppy is old enough to stay clean overnight, she will soon learn to relieve herself when she is let out of her crate into the yard or walked on a lead immediately upon being let out of the crate.

A crate is nothing more than a sturdy, safe enclosure, which you can buy or build, similar in shape to the containers used by airlines for animal transport. Try not to think about this process as putting the puppy in a cage, with all its negative connotations. It is *not* a jail cell or an instrument of punishment. In fact, many people find that puppies soon regard the crate as a place to retreat whenever they feel like having peace and quiet. They actually seem to appreciate possessing private space. Having a dog accustomed to being crated is also practical when you're traveling because it controls the animal's movement and offers restraint and protection if something unplanned happens. If you do a good job of crate training your puppy, you'll find that as he grows older, you can leave the crate door open and he will choose to go in his crate for naps and rest.

Many people buy a crate from a pet shop. If you cannot find a crate, ask your puppy's breeder if he or she has a spare crate or can tell you where to get one. You should aim for a clean, well-constructed enclosure with enough space for the puppy to rest comfortably, stand, and turn around.

If the puppy persists in using the crate as an outhouse, your problem may be excessive space. In that case, the puppy believes his sleeping requirements are well met on one end, so she might as well use the other end to relieve herself. You may be able to solve the problem by making a simple partition for the crate interior, progressively moving it back as the puppy grows.

In addition to their usefulness in housetraining, crates have an additional important benefit when it comes to raising your puppy. Crates keep puppies and older dogs new to your home *safe*. You should never, ever leave an untrained puppy in a situation where she can get into trouble or cause damage. Will a young, teething puppy chew on your furniture? You bet. Puppies need to chew and they don't yet know the rules about which things are acceptable for chewing. Worse than furniture are items like pencils or socks. Some objects, if eaten, can cause intestinal perforations or obstructions that can result in an expensive surgery, or worse yet, the death of your puppy. So don't offer any opportunities for your dog to get into trouble. Make sure you have a safe place to leave your puppy whenever you can't watch her. We're making this point as emphatically as possible so that you don't become disenchanted by misbehavior you could easily have prevented.

The key points to crate training include keeping feeding amounts and times consistent so that you can predict the puppy's elimination schedule; providing adequate exercise throughout the day to stimulate elimination when the puppy is outside; being disciplined about taking your puppy out at consistent, frequent intervals in the beginning; praising the puppy for eliminating outside; providing an outside break as the last thing you do before putting the puppy to bed at night; and taking the puppy out of the crate and straight outside immediately when you return home after being gone for a while.

Paper Training

Paper training is less ideal than crate training. If you choose paper training as a permanent method, your dog will be eliminating in your house on the paper. You will be smelling and handling soiled papers. If at all possible, you should try to get yourself in a position to get your dog on a schedule for going outside when nature calls.

In some cases, paper training is the only solution; in others, it must be used as a temporary solution. To paper train a dog, cover the entire floor of a room or confined space with several layers of newspaper and restrict the puppy to that area. (Other options in addition to using paper, for owners with small dogs who cannot get their dogs outside, include getting housetraining pads or a "litter box" designed for dogs, both of which are used in place of the paper.) Wait for her to use the papers, and then pick up the soiled sheets and replace them. Make sure you praise your puppy lavishly for using the papers. Continue in this fashion for a day or two. Then leave a small corner of the room bare, and hope the dog doesn't use this. If she does, put her on the papers, letting her know that this is the one and only place for her to go.

As soon as the dog seems to understand the paper concept, widen the bare area until you have left a papered space equivalent to about two full newspaper spreads. Allow your dog to use that area until she is ready to go outdoors. Begin walking with her until she learns that the street is the proper place for elimination, and then remove the papers. At that point, carefully observe the dog for indications that she needs to go out (she may search frantically for the papers) and walk her immediately. Until your puppy firmly understands the housebreaking idea, keep her absolutely confined to the paper-training area.

Whatever system you use for housetraining, "errorless training" should be your goal. Errorless training means that you do everything you can to prevent your dog from making a mistake. This requires diligence on your part. In the beginning, the schedule for going outside will involve very short times between trips. Gradually, the length of time between trips will lengthen. If you feed your dog at regular times, and maintain a schedule of trips outside, your puppy will be housetrained in no time.

Feeding

Here's another good reason to seek a puppy from a reputable breeder: You'll probably go home not only with a healthy dog, but also with a detailed description of diet, a temporary supply of food, and feeding instructions. If this information hasn't been offered, ask. It eases the puppy's transition to the new environment and helps prevent the gastric upset that may accompany an abrupt change of diet.

All puppies should be fed a diet designed for young, growing dogs (otherwise known simply as puppy food). Adult dog food is inappropriate at this phase of life, when puppies have special nutritional requirements for normal development. Feeding adult food will only rob your puppy of important nutrients, and the animal may not reach her full potential. Most name-brand puppy foods meet or exceed the nutritional requirements. Stay away from generic-label dog foods, no matter how attractive the lower price. The ingredients in generic dog food may not be in a form that is useful to the puppy. Stay with reputable name-brand dog food companies. In the pet food world, you get what you pay for.

Bearded Collie. *Chet Jezierski*

How much and how often to feed your puppy depends on her size and weight, as well as on other factors. Three feedings a day are usually adequate to meet nutritional demands. Hold to this schedule until the puppy is four to six months old and her stomach can accommodate larger amounts of food. Then you can cut back to two meals a day. Most dogs are fed once daily when they reach one year of age.

It is very important to prevent your puppy from becoming overweight, since obesity can lead to all sorts of health problems. Fat dogs are far too common. Try not to feed any table scraps, and keep the amount of treats to an absolute minimum. These are often the greatest source of unneeded calories. Weigh the puppy weekly and record her development, comparing her with published charts for the breed. You can then adjust the amount of food she's getting to conform with that for an average rate of growth. Plenty of exercise is important at this time, but make sure the puppy exercises on surfaces that are not too slippery or hard, to avoid possible injury.

English Springer Spaniel. *Mary Bloom*

As with socialization, a sincere breeder makes sure puppies are fed the right food in the proper amounts. Well-fed youngsters will also reflect this fact about themselves.

(A helpful hint: Weighing a dog, even a puppy who won't sit still, is easy. Just weigh yourself, then weigh yourself holding the puppy, and subtract the difference—that's the puppy.)

Try not to be too worried if your puppy skips a meal or picks at food occasionally. It could mean that she's ready to eliminate a feeding or that you've given her too much, in which case you can reduce the quantity of food you serve. Most dogs finish their meals quickly, although this is not always the case. If you want to discourage the development of picky habits, try to feed at regular times in regular amounts, and don't leave food down longer than 10 to 20 minutes. Fresh water, in a clean bowl, should be available at all times.

Types of Foods

Manufactured dog food is widely available in three types: canned (moist), semi-moist, and dry (kibble). You may also be able to obtain frozen dog food in your area.

Canned food is the most expensive to feed and dogs often find it most palatable. Be careful of "all meat" claims. Your dog should have a complete, balanced diet to fulfill all the nutritional needs, and meat alone won't do it.

Semi-moist foods are available in one-serving packets; usually the food is manufactured to look like chopped meat in one form or another.

Dry or kibble/biscuit dog foods are the most economical. Name brands offer a complete and balanced diet, providing everything your dog needs for her particular lifestyle. Dry food can be fed exactly as it comes from the bag. The good thing about feeding kibble dry is that it can be removed and used later if the dog does not finish a serving. Kibble can be moistened, either with water, canned food, or other supplements. Although unnecessary, such supplementation may make the food more palatable to your dog. Some owners think that dry dog food is boring and the dog will not like eating it. Keep in mind that for a dog, dry food provides a healthy, balanced diet.

Special foods are also commercially available for older dogs, overweight dogs, and dogs undergoing exceptional stress (lactating bitches, hunting dogs, and so on). When medically necessary, you can also purchase canned or dry prescription diets from veterinarians to feed dogs with kidney disease, heart disease, and other conditions.

As for bones, our best advice is caution. Some bones (such as poultry or pork bones) are absolutely discouraged, because they tend to splinter into needlelike fragments that can cause serious damage to the dog's mouth, throat, or intestinal tract. Any bone, in fact, once chewed into small pieces, can potentially obstruct the intestines. Ingested bone fragments can also produce a bout of uncomfortable constipation. If you are considering giving your dog bones of any type, proceed with caution. Do plenty of research on this topic and talk to your veterinarian.

There are other ways to satisfy a dog's craving to chew. A variety of toys and simulated "bones" are now available that are specifically designed for this purpose.

Bathing and Grooming

Young puppies are intrigued by life itself. From the moment their eyes open, they develop into world-class explorers. Puppies abandon themselves so joyously in their travels that cleanliness becomes difficult to enforce.

Don't get frustrated. Use this opportunity to get the puppy accustomed to being handled for bathing and grooming. In fact, start the day you get her home. Purchase the appropriate comb or brush for your breed's coat, and practice using it early and often. Make a habit of touching the puppy's feet and nails several times each day. This will help reduce the dog's anxiety at nail-trimming time. Also, run your hands over the coat, and gently fuss with the hair around the eyes and ears. These may need frequent cleaning or plucking in the future.

Many people wonder how often a dog needs to be bathed. The answer depends on the breed, the kind of life the dog leads, and whether she has a skin disorder. In general, dogs need only be bathed when dirty (or when a medicated shampoo is prescribed). More frequent shampooing may dry out their coats. When you employ proper shampoo and grooming techniques, as is the case with show dogs (who are bathed very often), the results can be quite spectacular.

Golden Retriever. *Diane Vasey*

Canine children are like human children when it comes to staying clean. Just ask any breeder about weaning a litter. And while young puppies are admittedly messy, they're also wonderfully funny about it. Take advantage of that untidy tyke and get him accustomed to grooming and bathing early on.

Grooming

Let's begin with basic grooming tools. Used correctly, these tools contribute significantly to the health of the skin and hair, and enhance a dog's general appearance.

1. *Brushes* come in a wide variety of sizes and styles.

    The bristle brush is an all-purpose brush that may be used on short-, medium-, double-, and long-coated breeds. The bristles can be made of nylon, natural material, or a combination of the two. The last is the most popular variety. It combines reasonable price with flexibility, as it can be used on many different coat types. All-nylon bristles are quite hard. They may break fragile hair or cause static electricity, so they are inappropriate for some types of coats. The softest type of brush is a natural bristle brush. It is also the most expensive.

    Pin brushes are usually used to groom long-haired breeds such as Afghans, Lhasa Apsos, Shih Tzu, and Yorkshire Terriers. They are also good for double-coated breeds like the Old English Sheepdog. A variety of sizes are available for easy brushing of small, medium, and large breeds. The pin palm brush, an oval rubber pad with pins that have rounded tips to prevent coat damage, is a special brush used to groom the face and legs of hard-coated terriers.

Another common type of brush is the slicker brush. The bent-wire teeth of the slicker brush are set close together to help remove mats and dead hair. Most come in three sizes: small, for Toy breeds; medium, for average-size breeds; and large, for heavy-coated or large breeds. Slicker brushes will take out large amounts of coat, which is good if you want to reduce the around-the-house accumulation from shedding. A slicker may not be the correct choice if you're trying to keep the maximum amount of coat on your dog for the show ring.

All-rubber brushes have flexible, short, soft bristles with rounded heads. They are fine for bringing out the shine in the coat of smooth-coated breeds or for removing dead hair without scratching the skin.

Helping you find the right grooming tools and supplies for your dog and showing you how to use them is the business of your puppy's breeder. Add another reason to the growing list of why it's smart to buy from a breeder.

2. *Combs* come in a wide variety of sizes and styles, with different tooth lengths and spacing. In general, fine-tooth combs are best used on soft, silky, or sparse hair. Medium-tooth combs are used for average coat textures, and coarse-tooth combs are good for dense or heavy coats. Some combs have close-set teeth on one end and wide-spaced teeth on the other end. The length of the teeth should depend on how far the comb needs to penetrate to reach the skin. Some combs have handles; others do not. The best combs are made of stainless steel or chrome-plated solid brass and have spring-tempered teeth with rounded tips to prevent skin irritation.

Bernese Mountain Dog. *Mary Bloom*

The younger a puppy is when its grooming routine is established, the better he will accept grooming as an adult. This becomes even more important for dogs of deep-coated or heavily groomed breeds, such as this Bernese Mountain Dog puppy.

Dandie Dinmont Terrier. *Mary Bloom*

As with other features of grooming, regular nail trimming is essential and must be started very early. Indeed, most breeders start trimming nails soon after birth. Accepting attention to nails and feet is important for all puppies to learn.

3. *Stripping implements* are used to groom show terriers and other harsh-coated breeds. In the broadest sense, stripping involves the removal of dead hair using a specialized grooming technique. Many purists insist on plucking with finger and thumb, and use stripping tools only to fine-tune their work. Clipping these breeds, which cuts off the ends of the hair without removing the dead undercoat, is undesirable because it tends to soften the texture of the coat and sometimes leads to faded coat color.

   There are also stripping combs, knives, dressers, and undercoat knives. Proper coat stripping is done over a period of weeks, depending on the coat texture, growth pattern, climate and humidity, among other things. For a better explanation on using stripping tools, consult your breed experts.

4. *Hair dryers* speed up the drying process and add a more finished look to the final grooming of long-haired dogs. Many types of hair dryers are on the market, priced from under a hundred dollars to more than a thousand. A few examples include portable or hand-held dryers; floor dryers, which are mounted on a stand; and cage dryers, which may be mounted with brackets on a cage door. Some coats do not require a dryer and are simply massaged with the

fingertips to maintain correct texture. A little research into your breed's coat characteristics should help you decide which dryer or drying process is best for your dog.

5. *Grooming tables,* for the person seriously interested in doing a proper grooming job, come in several sizes and shapes. The table should be sturdy and have a nonskid rubber top. Some are portable and can be folded up for storage. Others have hydraulic mechanisms to let you raise and lower the table. Most professional groomers attach a grooming post and loop to the table. The loop is placed around the dog's neck to keep it from moving around or jumping off the table, although the dog is never left unattended. Whatever type of table you use, grooming should be a comfortable experience for the dog. This shouldn't be too difficult if you allow her time to adjust to the procedure.

6. *Nail trimmers* come in a variety of types. The most common nail trimmer is the guillotine trimmer. To use one, insert the dog's nail into the opening of this metal tool above the cutting blade. When you squeeze the handles together, the cutting mechanism is activated. Other nail trimmer types are the scissors type and the safety nail trimmer, which is equipped with a safety stop near the cutting blade to limit the amount of nail trimmed. To prevent accidentally cutting the dog's nail too close and causing bleeding, some dog owners use nail files or electric "grinders." The grinder is a small sanding tool. Ideally, you are in the hands of a responsible breeder who can teach you how to do your dog's nail care. Otherwise, you could attend a dog show and meet someone locally who would be willing to teach you any skills you don't have.

Gordon Setter. *The AKC*

Heavy-coated dogs who compete in the show ring must undergo long grooming sessions. These dogs are often trained to lie on their sides during the process. This makes the whole procedure easier for both the dog and the groomer, and is a simple control exercise to teach any dog.

Nails seem to grow at different rates in different dogs. In any case, one rule holds true consistently: The nails must be kept short for the feet to remain healthy. Long nails interfere with the dog's gait, making walking awkward or painful. They can also break easily. This usually happens at the base of the nail, where blood vessels and nerves are located, and precipitates a trip to the veterinarian.

Another problem affects dogs whose overgrown nails curl toward the foot, eventually piercing the sensitive pads and causing deep pad infections. Dewclaws most frequently become overgrown, presumably because owners commonly overlook them. Many breeders routinely have dewclaws removed when puppies are a few days old. Check your puppy; if her dewclaws are intact, you must be sure to keep the nails short at all times. These problems can be easily prevented with regular nail care.

To begin, regularly stroke the puppy's feet, gently touching each toe in turn. Allow her to become accustomed to having this delicate part of the body handled, so she won't panic when you get down to business later.

Unfortunately, some dogs never adjust to having their nails trimmed. They need only see the clipper and they're squalling, long before you're anywhere near a nail. In that case, trimming nails becomes a two-person job: one person to hold the dog, the other to do the work. It can still be a test of wills. That's why you should accustom your young puppy to nail care. It increases the likelihood of good behavior throughout the dog's life.

Norfolk Terrier. *Mary Bloom*

Most terriers and a number of other breeds need to be stripped or plucked to maintain the texture and color of their coats. Special tools and techniques come into play, making hand-stripping a very artful, demanding practice. This is less important if the dog is to be a pet.

Greater Swiss Mountain Dog.
Mary Bloom

Unpigmented nails are simple to trim. If your dog has at least one unpigmented nail, examine it closely. You should see a small pink triangle extending from the base of the nail narrowing toward the tip. This triangle houses the blood supply and nerves, which you want to avoid when trimming the nail. Position the nail trimmer so that it clearly bypasses the pink area, and proceed to clip. That's all there is to nail trimming.

Of course, trimming nails is infinitely more challenging in dogs with black or pigmented nails. Because you can't see the pink part, you must estimate how much nail to clip. To be on the safe side, trim only the part of each nail that hooks downward. The trimmed nail should just clear the floor.

If you're absolutely unnerved at the thought of nail trimming, find a veterinarian or groomer to do it for you. This service usually costs very little and goes a long way in keeping your dog comfortable. You'll know if your dog's nails are too long when he walks across a hard surface such as a kitchen floor. If you hear the click, click, click of nails hitting the floor, consider it an indication that the nails should be shorter.

7. *Electric clippers* are specifically designed for home grooming or heavy-duty professional use. They come with a set of blades for different degrees of trimming. The blades are either snapped or screwed into place.

   Most dogs trimmed at home with electric clippers don't emerge with a salon-perfect coat. However, these practical tools make it relatively simple to keep many long-haired breeds comfortable, especially in summer.

8. *Scissors* and *shears* are used primarily for trimming and sculpting the coat. Many types are available; the type you need depends on the coat and the desired look. Check your breed literature for more specific instructions. *Warning:* You must be extremely careful, especially with puppies, if you decide to use these grooming tools. The dividing line between hair and skin is often difficult to see, particularly behind the ears and on the underside. A costly mistake can happen in the blink of an eye. If your puppy resists your efforts, don't take a chance. Leave this job to a professional groomer.

How to Bathe a Dog

The average dog should be bathed as seldom as possible, only when clearly dirty or smelly. Frequent washing tends to remove natural oils, and may cause the coat to become dry and harsh. There are exceptions, however. Dogs who suffer from skin conditions sometimes respond to frequent treatments with a prescription shampoo. Regular bathing or dipping may be necessary during certain times of the year to combat fleas. In any case, here's a primer on dog bathing.

Before shampooing, thoroughly brush the dog to remove dirt, dandruff, and dead hair. Brushing also helps to distribute natural oils through the coat. Short- or smooth-coated dogs need only a slight stroking with a bristle brush. Take a moment to massage the skin and coat with your fingertips; this helps loosen dead hair and debris (it probably helps relax the dog as well).

Preparing a long-haired dog for bathing is slightly more complicated, because this type of coat is often matted. You must remove mats *before shampooing* or else they trap soap residue. Mats are also harder to remove after a bath.

If there are just a few mats, gently tease them apart with your fingers, the teeth of a comb, or a dematting tool. Keep a firm grasp on the hair nearest to the dog's body to prevent pulling on the skin as you work. Soaking the mat in a detangling lotion may also help.

In the case of numerous mats, however, the kindest thing to do is to clip the hair short—and then closely monitor the coat in the future. Mats can form surprisingly fast in places where there is natural body friction, such as the base of the ears and around the joints. Also, long-haired breeds shedding out of the soft puppy coat may be especially prone to matting. Whether you like it or not, if your dog's coat gets matted, it's because you neglected it.

Before you take scissors to your dog's mats, be warned. Many people inadvertently cut their dog's skin while trying to cut out mats. If you must snip, try teasing a comb under the mat so that the teeth rest safely between the skin and the tangle. Then cut the mat off outside the comb. This will create an unsightly gouge in the coat, but at least the mat problem will be solved.

Once all mats are removed and the hair is well brushed, you're ready to place the dog in a tub or sink, depending on size, and start scrubbing.

First, select a shampoo designed *for dogs*, not people. Such products are formulated to clean and condition the dog's more alkaline skin and hair. Baby shampoo or a coconut-oil shampoo will do in a pinch. You may choose to gently insert a cotton ball in your dog's ears, and place a dab of mild ophthalmic ointment or mineral oil in its eyes. You'd best don a plastic apron to protect your clothes. Now adjust the water temperature, put the dog in the tub, and you're ready to go.

Bathing a dog is much easier if the faucet is equipped with a hose, especially one with a spray nozzle. Wet the hair thoroughly. You can start at either the head or the tail, unless you're using a flea shampoo, in which case you'll want to begin at the head and leave a ring of shampoo on the neck to prevent fleas from fleeing to the head for refuge.

Shetland Sheepdog. *Mary Bloom*

Rinse the hair first to remove as much dirt as possible. Then apply a small amount of shampoo to the back and work up a lather. Don't use too much shampoo, or rinsing will be difficult. Massage the shampoo well all over the body, unless the dog has long hair, in which case you will want to squeeze the shampoo gently through the strands to avoid tangling up the hairs. Don't forget to shampoo the areas under the legs and tail, as well as the head.

Getting water all the way down to skin level requires considerable effort in breeds with heavy coats. In many cases, this is a direct consequence of selective breeding to create an animal with a coat capable of protection against the elements. Unfortunately, this means more work at bath time. Be certain to thoroughly douse the dog and work shampoo all the way through to the skin.

Rinsing, too, is more of a chore with a heavily coated breed. Rinsing shampoo from the coat is simpler if your hose attachment releases a fine spray. Check the water temperature again and begin to rinse, starting at the head and finishing at the tail. Make sure all of the soap, especially on the underside of the dog, is gone. You may need to repeat the bathing process two or even three times, depending on the coat length, type, and degree of soiling before cleanliness is achieved. For best results, do not fill the tub or sink while rinsing.

And bather, beware: As soon as a dog gets wet, she will have an insidious, devil-may-care urge to shake herself dry. Even a small terrier can spray enough water all around to necessitate having a mop handy. If the weather permits, outdoor bathing will greatly minimize the mess of dog washing. Dogs are less apt to shake if you maintain physical contact with them until you're ready to either grab a towel or take a quick step back.

When you're convinced that you have completely rinsed the dog, squeeze excess water from her coat and wrap her in an absorbent towel. Take her out of the washtub and blot as dry as possible. Try not to rub the coat dry, since this may only produce tangles. Then let the dog dry in the sun or turn to an electric hair dryer for a quick finish.

Dealing with Skunk Odor

It's true that tomato juice, applied full strength to the coat, deadens the obnoxious odor of skunk. Nothing works 100 percent, however. Repeated baths (outdoors, if at all possible) may be necessary. If you share your habitat with many skunks, ask your breeder or local dog club for suggestions on coping with the problem.

English Toy Spaniel. *Mary Bloom*

Special bathing products sold by veterinarians and pet stores can also help eliminate skunk odor. Eventually, the lingering aroma dissipates by itself. Forget about saving the dog's collar, leash, or other accoutrements worn at the time of the incident, though. Skunk odor will waft from these articles far longer than you can bear, so just consider them casualties and retire them to the trash.

Brushing Your Dog's Teeth

Dental hygiene is often ignored in the dog. The outcome? Consider what your teeth might look and feel like after months, years, or even a lifetime of neglect. They'd be a wreck, and you'd be miserable. Yes, canine teeth also need frequent brushing to prevent gum disease and early tooth loss, as well as just plain foul breath.

Despite the popular conception, dog biscuits and bones alone do not keep the teeth clean and healthy. Although some veterinarians feel that gnawing on these hard substances has benefit, it does not completely prevent the buildup of plaque and tartar, which, unless removed, can lead to gum inflammation, tooth root abscesses, and other oral problems. That's the simple truth.

You should brush your dog's teeth at least once or twice a week, more often if possible. As with grooming, acclimation is best started early in the puppy's life.

To make a toothbrush, fold a square gauze pad loosely around the tip of your index finger. Or you can use a small, soft child's toothbrush or buy a special toothbrush from a veterinarian. Dip the toothbrush or gauze pad in a toothpaste designed for dogs (human formulations can upset the dog's stomach) or into a paste made of baking soda and water. Next, vigorously scrub the outside surfaces of the teeth, especially the rear teeth. With the gauze pad, try to gently massage the gums. It is not necessary to brush the interior surfaces of the teeth.

Norwegian Elkhound. *Mary Bloom*

Just as with people, a dog's teeth are meant to last a lifetime. A regular routine of dental hygiene will keep your dog's mouth clean, healthy, and trouble-free, and most of the work can be done at home by the owner.

Your veterinarian should check your dog's mouth for tooth or gum disease during annual checkups. The most common problem, tartar accumulation, resembles yellow or brown cement deposits along the gumline or in the crevices of the teeth. Despite your best efforts, a proper dental cleaning under general anesthesia may need to be performed periodically in a veterinarian's office.

Certain breeds commonly retain their baby teeth, especially the canines. In that case, duplicate sets of teeth will appear in the dog's mouth after approximately six months of age. Retained baby teeth can cause malocclusion, because they prevent adult teeth from growing into their correct position. Retained baby teeth are often extracted by a veterinarian.

Anal Sacs

Finally, a word about anal sacs. These two sacs are located in the muscle tissue on either side of the anus at the five and seven o'clock positions. An intensely malodorous secretion, usually brownish and watery in appearance, resides within the sacs.

The anal sac fluid, which emerges through two tiny ducts, serves an unknown purpose in the dog. According to different theories, the release of anal sac fluid may help dogs mark territory, show fear or a sign of trouble, or enable them to distinguish one another's sexual identity. Whatever their purpose, the anal sacs of most dogs can be ignored throughout life. Other dogs, however, are bothered by periodic anal sac problems. They show it by madly dragging their hindquarters across the floor or biting and licking at the tail area. These dogs need to have their anal sacs manually emptied (expressed). Some dogs might need to have the sacs surgically removed.

How often may your dog's anal sacs need to be expressed? This depends on whether your dog is one who suffers from bouts of impaction or from actual anal sac infections. Some dogs need monthly attention, while others can go several months or a lifetime without a problem. If you see your dog doing something that suggests a problem with the anal sacs, discuss the signs and symptoms of the problems as soon as possible with your veterinarian.

Your veterinarian will examine your dog and decide if you need to learn to empty your dog's anal sacs or if a medical intervention is necessary. While owners can be easily taught to empty the anal sacs at home, a veterinarian should first decide if this should be done for your particular dog. If you will be doing this, you should get a lesson from your vet. Expressing the anal sacs is a simple task for someone who knows what they are doing, but if you don't know what you are doing and you apply excessive force, you may rupture the delicate sacs. Having your veterinarian involved during the assessment of your dog's potential problem is important because sometimes, in addition to the anal sacs being impacted, there is an infection that needs to be treated with antibiotics.

Fortunately, most dogs never have anal sac trouble, but for those who do, the preceding discussion may be helpful.

Choosing and Working with a Veterinarian

You and your puppy will make frequent visits to the veterinarian in the first few months, so it's extremely important to find someone you trust. If you're not familiar with the practitioners in your area, your breeder is. Word of mouth is also a good place to start. Listen closely to what people say about their experiences with local veterinarian. What pleases or distresses one person may have the opposite effect on you.

For instance, your neighbor may dislike a large clinic nearby because she never seems to see the same doctor twice. She wants a smaller practice, perhaps one or two doctors, where she and her dog receive personal attention.

You, however, may discover that the clinic has lots of doctors because it is a teaching facility. Its senior veterinarians have advanced training, are highly skilled, and know the latest medical information—they must, because they pass the information on to the interns and residents who are part of the examination, diagnostic, and treatment processes. This degree of sophistication may be exactly what makes you feel secure. To each his own.

Wherever you go, you must respect and feel comfortable with the veterinarian who cares for your dog's health. Don't forget that the animal, though she broadcasts many clues to the educated eye, can't speak for herself. This makes you a vital part of the examination process. Only you can relate the important details of your pet's health. When it comes to illness, only you can describe the problem's onset, signs, and so on. You must effectively communicate with your dog's veterinarian, not feel intimidated or shy. If an individual's personality puts you off or otherwise hinders your ability to tell the full story, find another vet.

Useful things you might want to know about local veterinarians include whether emergency service is provided at night and on weekends, or whether an emergency clinic in the vicinity provides emergency coverage. Some veterinarians hold evening or weekend appointments; perhaps this fits in with your lifestyle. Furthermore, if you intend to travel frequently, ask if the animal hospital accepts boarders and inspect the boarding facilities.

It's important to know whether the practice you're considering is "full service," meaning that the practitioners can handle a broad spectrum of cases. Are specialists available for consultation, or are certain procedures referred to specialists elsewhere? Don't be embarrassed to inquire about the type of equipment on hand. For example, are x-ray machinery, ultrasound, and dental equipment available? Many up-to-date practices now employ a computer system for organized record keeping and for sending you timely reminders for vaccinations or other important procedures. This may represent a major convenience to you.

Although you may not have the opportunity to meet the doctors, try to visit a clinic in which you're interested. At least you can form a general impression of the facility and its staff.

Beginning a Program of Good Health

The following sections walk you through important good-health practices for your puppy.

Vaccinations

Most puppies receive their first vaccinations at eight weeks of age, although some breeders or pet stores vaccinate their puppies a few weeks early. The first vaccination is usually a "combination" shot, intended to produce immunity against five serious canine diseases: distemper; hepatitis; leptospirosis; parvovirus; and parainfluenza. Different veterinarians use different vaccination schedules, but in

The Brittany is named for its place of origin in northern France. A compact, medium-size hunting dog, he is rugged, strong, and energetic. *Diane Vasey*

The Pomeranian is a member of the Spitz family, descended from Arctic sled dogs. Today, their diminutive size, docile temperament, lively spirit, and sturdiness make them great pets and companions. *Mary Bloom*

The French Bulldog is a muscular dog of heavy bone, with an active expression, and is of medium or small size. He has an alert, curious, and interested expression.
Mary Bloom

The Mastiff is a giant shorthaired dog, with a heavy head and short muzzle. His temperament is a combination of grandeur and good nature, courage, and docility. Dignity is the Mastiff's correct demeanor.
Mary Bloom

The Rottweiler is a large, robust, and powerful dog. His build connotes great strength, agility, and endurance. By nature, he is calm, confident, and courageous. *Mary Bloom*

The Yorkshire Terrier became a fashionable pet in the late-Victorian era and continues to hold on to that same popularity today. Although a toy, and at times a pampered one, he possesses a true Terrier spirit. *Mary Bloom*

The Collie existed hundreds of years ago as herding dogs tending flocks of sheep in Scotland and northern England. A smart dog with natural herding and protecting abilities, he makes a great family pet and is especially fond of children. *Mary Bloom*

The Scottish Deerhound resembles a Greyhound, but he is rough-coated and is larger in size and bone. The natural grace, dignity, and beauty of the Deerhound made him a popular subject of art. *Mary Bloom*

The Bulldog, who originated in the British Isles, has a general appearance and attitude that suggests stability, vigor, and strength. By nature, he is kind, resolute, and courageous, while pacific and dignified in behavior.
Mary Bloom

The Boxer descended from various larger breeds, some related to the Mastiffs. While playful and patient with family, he is strong and defensive. His intelligence and loyal affection make him a most popular companion.
Mary Bloom

The Cardigan Welsh Corgi is the Corgi with the tail. He is believed to have descended from the same ancestors as the Dachshund. *Mary Bloom*

The Soft Coated Wheaten Terrier is a medium-sized dog, but one of the largest of the Terrier breeds. The Wheaten is a happy, steady dog who conducts himself gaily and with great confidence. *The American Kennel Club*

The Old English Sheepdog is a sturdy herder of sheep and cattle that English farmers have valued for many years. His nature is that of an adaptable, intelligent dog, possessing an even disposition. *Mary Bloom*

The German Shorthaired Pointer is a versatile sporting dog of medium size. He has a keen enthusiasm for work and is friendly, intelligent, and always willing to please. *The American Kennel Club*

The American Foxhound, although bred for the specific purpose of chasing fox, loves children and adults alike, and can make a lovable pet. He is smaller in bone than his English cousins. *The American Kennel Club, photo by Kent and Donna Dannen*

The Keeshond is a hardy breed of medium size and with an alert carriage and intelligent expression. He has been respected for centuries as an ideal family companion and sensible watchdog. *Mary Bloom*

The Miniature Pinscher moves with a hackney-like gait. Intelligent and alert, he is happiest when treated like a standard-sized dog. *Steve Eltinge*

general, this DHLPP shot is repeated twice more, at two- to four-week intervals. Until the three-shot series is completed, it's best to isolate your puppy from unfamiliar dogs, since the proper degree of immunity is not yet established. Once the puppy has received the last of the three shots, usually by 12 to 16 weeks of age, it's safe for her to come in contact with strange dogs. The vaccination is updated with an annual booster.

Most veterinarians administer the first rabies vaccination when a dog is six months old. The next rabies shot is given in a year. Ask your veterinarian if the vaccination needs to be boosted each year or once every three years throughout the dog's adult life. The rabies vaccination is an absolute requirement for licensing your dog. Many towns offer a free rabies clinic yearly. Check with your town officials.

Two other vaccinations are available for dogs at the present time; these prevent tracheobronchitis (kennel cough) and the coronavirus infection, which can cause a hemorrhagic gastroenteritis. These vaccinations are usually administered twice, spaced a few weeks apart. Ask your veterinarian whether these are considered an important part of your dog's disease protection.

Pug. *Mary Bloom*

Kuvasz. *Mary Bloom*

Veterinary science makes constant strides forward in its understanding of animal health. Today, your puppy can be protected by sophisticated vaccinations that provide potent protection against diseases that earlier in the century wiped out whole populations of dogs. With good management and a sensible program of boosters, most dogs can be expected to live long, happy, healthful lives.

In the late 1990s, a vaccine was approved for animals for the prevention of Lyme Disease. Lyme Disease is an infectious disease caused by a spiral-shaped bacterium called *Borrelia burgdorferi.* The disease is transmitted to humans and animals by the bite of a deer tick. Lyme Disease has been reported in almost every state, and the risk of contracting the disease is greater in dogs and people who spend time in or near wooded areas. In dogs, Lyme Disease is diagnosed by blood tests. There are a number of symptoms, including fever, lameness, and lack of appetite. Veterinarians treat Lyme Disease with antibiotics and, if detected early enough, the prognosis is good. There are some differences of opinion about the benefits and risks of the vaccine, so you may want to consult with your veterinarian to determine whether you should vaccinate your dog for Lyme Disease.

Gastrointestinal Parasites

The majority of puppies contract some form of internal parasite either before or shortly after birth. Although this may sound repulsive to you, it's a normal part of being a dog. There is no need to be excessively concerned, provided you have your puppy checked and treated promptly. Left untreated, intestinal parasites can cause serious harm.

Therefore, it's essential to bring along a small, fresh sample of your puppy's stool when you make your first veterinary visit. When the stool is dissolved, eggs or parasites from this sample will be clearly visible under a microscope. Do not assume that your puppy has no intestinal parasites simply because no worms have shown up in the stool. Adult worms often live exclusively within the intestinal tract; the tiny eggs they release serve as the only clue to their existence. Furthermore, other internal parasites, even as mature organisms, never reach a size visible to the naked eye. Let your veterinarian discover which type, if any, of these parasites inhabits your puppy's system and treat it accordingly.

Heartworms

Another parasite you'll learn about during your puppy's first visit to the veterinarian is heartworm.

The microscopic heartworm initially gains entry to the dog's body through the bite of an infected mosquito. Later, adult worms inhabit the heart's chambers where, now several inches long, they present a life-threatening problem. We'll go over heartworms in more detail in Chapter 8. For now, suffice it to say that veterinarians dispense preventative drugs to protect dogs whenever mosquitoes are active in the local environment. In some parts of the country, this is virtually year-round. Elsewhere, it is a seasonal problem. In all cases, however, owners should have their dogs' blood tested yearly to confirm that heartworm infection has not occurred. If a dog tests positive, he can be treated, but the treatment and its aftermath are extremely stressful.

Spaying or Neutering

Your veterinarian should initiate a discussion about spaying or neutering at the time of your first appointment, months in advance of the actual surgery. If he or she doesn't, then inquire. It's a good time to start thinking about whether you want to spay or neuter your pet for preventative health care, birth control, and to avoid some potentially undesirable behavior. Remember, however, that these surgical procedures render a dog ineligible to compete in the show ring. Even though spayed or neutered dogs cannot compete in conformation shows (one of the purposes of which is to select the best specimens of the breed for reproduction), dogs who have been spayed or neutered are welcome in many AKC events, including Canine Good Citizen® tests, obedience, and agility. Spayed or neutered dogs may compete in all Field Trials (with the exception of Beagle and Basset Field Trials), as well as Coonhound, Lure Coursing, Earthdog, Herding, Hunt, and Tracking Events. They may also compete in Junior Showmanship.

Many breeders offer pet-quality puppies for sale with the stipulation that the dogs be neutered or spayed when they reach the appropriate age. This is the breeder's way of insuring breed improvement, by allowing only high-quality dogs to reproduce. You, of course, think your puppy is absolutely perfect. And he is—for you, and as a pet, but perhaps not as a model for future members of the breed.

Possibly the best reason to have your female spayed while she is young (usually around six months of age) is for her health benefit. Mammary gland cancer is much more common in an unspayed (intact) female. If your puppy is spayed before her first heat (at six months, for example), her risk of developing breast tumors is substantially reduced. The odds are still in her favor if she is spayed after her first heat. The longer you wait to spay, the less the benefit in reducing her risk of breast cancer. This is why it is important to have her spayed early in life.

Other reasons? The surgery itself, complete removal of the uterus and both ovaries, is ordinarily quicker and less hemorrhagic in immature females, so the risk of complications is reduced. Owners are spared the stress of having to confine the female who, when she comes into season, sends out enticing messages to male dogs in the vicinity. Furthermore, spaying eliminates the possibility of unwanted pregnancy, as well as the regular heat period when dogs leave blood-tinged stains on carpets and furniture. Finally, the potential for infections, cancers, and other problems involving the uterus and ovaries are eliminated when these organs are removed.

Ibizan Hound. *Mary Bloom*

If you will not be showing or breeding your dog, arrange to have your pet spayed or neutered. Ask your veterinarian when it will be appropriate and act accordingly. Your dog will be just as lovely a companion, maybe better.

Diseases of the male reproductive organs related to the presence of male hormones also exist. Although neutering represents an advantage as far as prevention is concerned, this is not usually the primary reason owners have their dogs neutered.

Most people want their dog to be neutered because they think it helps make him a better pet. This may be true for the following reasons:

1. Intact male dogs can act aggressively toward other dogs and people because they are trying to protect and control their territory. In the male dog mind, "territory" may be your property, his toys, females in heat, a bowl of food, and so on. This type of behavior is unacceptable to most people and may be strongly influenced by the dog's hormones. Neutering a dog with aggressive tendencies at an early age may reduce these problems. Neutering is also recommended for aggressive older dogs, although the chances for success are less certain.

2. A neutered dog has less temptation to roam. He probably won't embarrass you at important dinner parties by seeking romance with your company's legs. And just as important, he won't contribute to the already burgeoning population of homeless puppies, something we should all be concerned about.

Let's face it. Spaying and neutering dogs who are not intended for breeding or for the show ring is the smart thing to do. If your dog is a pet who you will not be showing in conformation shows, it makes sense to choose spaying or neutering as a means of having a happier, healthier pet.

Afghan Hound. *Mary Bloom*

Owning a dog is a privilege as well as a pleasure. The conscientious owner knows that with the privilege comes the responsibility of keeping the dog under control.

∎ 4 ∎

LIVING WITH
YOUR DOG

Living happily with your dog means in part that you and your dog are welcome in your community. You'll want to teach and manage your dog in such a way that shows you are a good neighbor. Part of being a good neighbor is making sure that your dog never infringes on the rights of others. Responsible dog owners don't let their dogs run at large, they have a secure outdoor fencing system, and they don't let their dogs bark excessively. When traveling, responsible dog owners take good care of hotel rooms and campgrounds. In places where dogs will not benefit from the activity and might make it less enjoyable for others, responsible dog owners find options for leaving the dog at home, such as kennels that can be trusted to provide high-quality care.

Being a Good Neighbor

Dogs are a part of our families, neighborhoods, and communities. As a dog owner, you have a serious responsibility. You are responsible for making your dog a good neighbor. Good neighbors never infringe upon the rights of other people, and they don't make themselves a nuisance or a menace.

Left to their own devices, dogs naturally do things like destroy or defecate on someone's lawn, chase other animals, or have long, loud barking sessions about the squirrels in the backyard. These are not *bad* behaviors; these are natural canine behaviors, and dogs will do them unless they are properly trained and supervised. This is your responsibility. Certainly you don't want your dog's behavior to become a point of contention between otherwise compatible neighbors.

To begin with, no dog should be allowed to roam throughout the neighborhood. Most people are reluctant to confront the owner of an offending dog, but no one appreciates a trespassing canine. Dogs lacking human supervision will often leave some degree of destruction in their path, and you are liable for your pet's activities. Don't let bad feelings start because you have given your dog a free rein.

Furthermore, in addition to breaking leash laws you may have in your area, you put your dog's life at risk every time you allow him such freedom. Your pet may attack or be attacked by other animals—wild (think about rabies) or domesticated. Chances are, at some point, the dog could be hit and perhaps killed by a car. A free-roaming dog is more susceptible to picking up parasites and disease. And he may simply disappear one day, leaving you to wonder about his fate. Sadly, these are common occurrences.

If you want to keep your dog outdoors for a part of the day, an exercise run or a sturdy fence around your yard is mandatory. Ideally, if your dog is a barker, your neighbors live a good distance away. However, in the densely populated urban and suburban areas in which most of us live, it is simply unacceptable to permit a dog to bark endlessly. You are going to have extremely unhappy neighbors. Breaking the barking habit can be a real problem; you can try working with a trainer to come up with a solution, or you may simply have to keep the dog indoors. Certainly, it is unfair to make other people suffer while you're away.

Rhodesian Ridgeback. *The AKC*

In today's lifestyle, part of being a thoughtful dog owner is keeping your dog on his own property. A fenced yard or exercise area and on-leash walks are better for people and dogs than allowing animals to roam at large. Dogs should always be a substantial pleasure, never a potential menace.

Wire Fox Terrier. *The AKC*

Every well cared–for dog has the potential to be a canine goodwill ambassador. From puppyhood on, all dogs should be raised and trained to promote the real and important image of dogs as our best friends.

Remember, barking is both natural for dogs and a learned behavior in certain situations. If you are going to correct unwanted barking, you must catch the dog in the act. You cannot correct undesirable behavior unless the dog is actually caught in the act of performing it. One of the best solutions for barking is to put the behavior "on cue." This means you teach the dog the commands "bark" and "no bark." If the dog is barking in the house when someone comes down the driveway, you might teach an alternative behavior, such as going to the door and sitting in wait. Finally, when the dog is barking excessively outside because there is a dog in the yard next door, you may have to structure outside times so that you are present to provide playtime and supervision.

Many dogs dig under or leap over fences, so you will have to discover your dog's style of escape artistry and foil it. Ideally, your dog will be a family member and will have, as an option, time she can spend in the house. However, if for some reason your dog spends a good deal of time outside unsupervised, you may find yourself installing a fence that is partially buried under the ground or one that has additional wiring on the top. You'll have to decide which fence modifications suit you, based on the particular type of Houdini-esque skills your dog exhibits.

Water and shelter must be made available for dogs who are kept out-doors, especially in very hot or cold weather. Be sure that the water supply has not evaporated or frozen. No matter what kind of coat your dog has, shade must be provided from the sun during summer months. Obviously, some dogs with thin or short coats were not designed for living outdoors in areas where winter weather can be harsh. If your dog is sufficiently coated and you want him to spend time outdoors in win-ter, he still needs adequate shelter from moisture, cold, and wind.

In fact, the vast majority of companion dogs live almost exclusively indoors. The chances are good your dog will, too. Therefore, for many dogs, most contact with neighbors occurs from the end of a leash. This is when you can best show off your dog's ability to be a good neighbor. The clearest way to demonstrate that your dog has manners is to make sure he knows the basic commands: sit, stay, down, come, and heel (see Chapter 5). If you want to show others that your dog has good manners, consider taking your dog through the Canine Good Citizen® Test (see Chapter 5) and earning a certificate from The American Kennel Club. Also, remember to exercise *your* command of good man-ners by removing and disposing properly of your dog's feces. Whether or not this practice is required by law in your area, it makes for a cleaner neighborhood as well as appreciative neighbors.

Exercising Your Dog

The amount of exercise your dog needs depends on age, health, breed, and temperament. In general, Sporting, Hound, Working, and Herding breeds appreciate and require more exercise than other breeds, especially the larger dogs. In fact, if denied sufficient exercise, they may become frustrated and turn to destructiveness as a way of venting energy. How much time you have for dog-related activities is obviously something to be considered before you decide on a breed.

Young animals always seem more keen on vigorous exercise than older animals. In the first few months of life, don't be surprised if your puppy has tremendous spurts of energy, followed by extensive rest peri-ods. This is natural for her stage of life.

Maintaining a regular exercise schedule for your dog as he grows will help him stay fit and healthy. Compared to their ancestors, today's dogs are out of condition; many are considerably overweight by the time they reach early adulthood because of too much rich food and too little exercise. Obesity, in turn, leads to all sorts of problems. Keep tabs on your dog's weight and muscle tone. You should be able to just feel the dog's ribs as you stand over her and pass your hands down the rib cage.

Golden Retrievers. *Mary Bloom*

The essential matter of exercise. Dogs are usually active individuals and, given the opportunity, will exercise themselves or join you in physical pursuits in a number of ways.

What kinds of exercises can you do with your dog? Walking is only the start. If your dog is well trained, she can be taken off-lead in approved public areas like parks and fields, and work off as much steam as he likes. Always check first with public authorities to see what the local laws allow. Perhaps you have friends, relatives, or acquaintances whose property you can use for the same purpose.

You can also take your dog hiking, jogging, or swimming. Dogs enjoy chasing balls and retrieving sticks or toys. For more structured activity, maybe you'd like to get involved in obedience, tracking work, or hunting with your dog. Field training, agility, and Lure Coursing are especially good for providing dogs with ample exercise. The AKC can help put you in touch with representatives of local clubs devoted to these activities.

Above all, dogs just want to spend time with the people they love. It's up to you to make that time count.

Some animals can't tolerate a lot of exercise because of hip dysplasia, arthritis, or other medical conditions. These problems may occur even in young dogs. Many owners like the idea of having a dog who will jog with them. Some pet dogs are not physically suited for running long distances. If exercise makes your dog sore and lame, or if he collapses or fatigues easily, have your vet examine the animal.

Traveling with Your Dog

If you and your family are looking forward to taking trips with your new puppy, it's best to prepare for the event right from the start.

Car sickness is fairly common in dogs. You can help your puppy overcome this by letting him adjust to car rides early in life. While he's still a few months old, take the puppy out and sit with him in the car.

There's no need to start the engine yet. Just let the animal get used to the signs and smells of the automobile. Later there will be less cause for alarm. Many dogs see the inside of a car only on those rare occasions when they are driven to the veterinarian. Few dogs enjoy that particular experience. Of course they're going to panic when the car door closes behind them!

After a few sessions of sitting in the car, the puppy is ready for short trips. Plan to take your puppy out before eating, so he has an empty stomach. You may want to begin by circling the block a few times. Soothe the puppy's excitement or anxiety during these rides, and reward afterward with praise and treats. Before long, the puppy should think car rides are another part of normal life, and she will be ready for extended trips without incident.

We recommend using the crate when you travel with a dog. Crates can provide protection from serious injury or prevent escape in the event you are involved in an accident. Furthermore, they can prevent trouble by keeping the dog away from the driver's lap and feet.

No matter how much your dog seems to enjoy it, never allow a dog to ride with her head sticking out the car window. For one thing, eye injuries are likely. Furthermore, you risk losing your dog this way—to escape (even the smallest dog can leap out the window in a flash) or death from trauma once they hit the road. Better safe than sorry; keep your dog away from open windows while you're driving.

German Shepherd Dog. *Mary Bloom*

Cairn Terrier. *The AKC*

Traveling with a dog by air is another consideration. Unless your dog is a seasoned traveler, she will probably find flying stressful, so you may want to think twice before subjecting her to the friendly skies. Each airline has its own rules and regulations for canine passengers. You must check with the airline well in advance of your trip. All will require a regulation crate, however, and some sort of documentation from a veterinarian certifying the dog is in good health. Airlines are careful about extreme temperatures, and they will not fly dogs when temperatures are not within a specified range. Even though the plane itself may not be a problem, during extreme weather conditions, airlines do not want to be responsible for dogs in crates who are waiting to be shipped.

Some people prefer to tranquilize their dogs prior to travel. Bear in mind, however, that tranquilization may not be necessary. In fact, because of certain medical considerations, tranquilization may be contraindicated for your dog. Ask your veterinarian for her advice in seeing your dog safely to the destination.

Finding a Place to Stay

Although it can be challenging to find motels, hotels, or campgrounds that accept dogs without question these days, you'll find, with a little planning, that there are plenty of pet-friendly accommodations. Always find out in advance whether pets are welcome at your expected destination. The American Automobile Association (AAA) publishes a list of pet-friendly accommodations in its special book on traveling with pets. Some establishments make the decision based on the dog's size or whether you will keep him crated. Again, you can avoid disappointment by checking first.

If your pet *is* given the green light, respect the privacy of other guests by keeping your dog as quiet as possible. Never leave the dog unattended, since many dogs become anxious when left alone in a strange place and bark or destroy property. When you're in for the night, confine the dog to the crate. Or, if your dog will get on the bed, make sure your dog is absolutely clean and bring a sheet from home to cover the bedspread. Don't give your dog a bath in the hotel tub. Keep in mind that the towels provided are for you, not the dog. Try to prevent any possibility of "accidents." Remember, the fate of future travelers with their dogs rests on how well you and yours respect the rights of the establishment. In heavily visited tourist areas, it can be somewhat more time consuming to find hotels that will accept dogs.

Finally, if the hotel keeper hasn't already told you, ask where you may walk your dog. The management may not appreciate its well-kept grounds used for this purpose. In any case, be sure to scoop up after your dog.

Boarding

Sometimes it's not possible to travel with your dog. Also, bringing the dog on vacation may hamper the activity of the rest of the family. It might be much smarter on your part to board your dog at a reliable kennel. If you decide to leave your dog in a kennel, here are some points to consider.

First of all, have friends who are dog owners recommend a particular boarding kennel. Ask if they thought the kennel was clean, well organized, and respected any special requests regarding their dog's food or housing. If they didn't like a kennel, find out why. Did the dog contract an illness at the kennel? Did she come home dirty or bring back fleas? When it comes to choosing a kennel for your dog, the best advice is to take the recommendation of someone you know who has had a satisfactory experience.

Then make an unannounced stop at the boarding kennel and ask to see the facility. The staff should not find your arrival disturbing and should honor, within reason, your request to view the premises. Expecting total spotlessness is unrealistic, but the runs should be clean, and every dog should have clean water. Foul odors of any kind should not pervade the air. Make a mental note of how the animals, in general, look to you.

Well-run kennels take a minute to check for fleas when dogs arrive and just before they go home; flea problems are immediately treated. They require that all dogs have up-to-date vaccinations, for their own protection and for the protection of other dogs. Many kennels require proof of a current kennel cough vaccination before they will admit a dog. The kennel operators may insist that you submit a certificate from your veterinarian stating all of these requirements are met, so be prepared well ahead of time. These rules may seem inconvenient to you, but they are in the best interest of your dog.

Kennels should also allow you to bring food or toys from home, and should provide canned food instead of dry when asked. Administering regular medication to dogs may or may not present a problem at a boarding kennel. If it does, it might be better to board your dog at a veterinary hospital, where qualified personnel will see to the job.

It's imperative to leave an emergency number where you can be reached, as well as the name and number of your veterinarian. If you are not able to provide an emergency phone number where you can be reached, leave written instructions empowering someone at the kennel or a specific veterinarian to authorize necessary medical treatment. It's also a good idea to compose a brief medical history of your animal and leave it with the kennel staff, just in case.

Harrier. *Mary Bloom*

▪ 5 ▪

TRAINING YOUR DOG

Y ou can't live happily with a dog unless he's trained. It's that simple, and it really doesn't matter whether your canine is a four-pound Toy or a 104-pound Working breed. An untrained dog is an invitation to problems. A dog who won't come when you call is always in danger.

You can't blame the dog. If you don't train your dog, you are at fault. No one else. In fact, if you're not prepared to properly train your dog, you probably shouldn't get one in the first place. Everyone who decides to own a dog needs to make a commitment to be a responsible dog owner. A key part of responsible dog ownership is providing your dog with the necessary training to be a well-behaved community member.

Now for the good news: Dogs are easily trained and the resources are readily available to you to help you train your dog. The fact that dogs are easily trained is probably the reason dogs have long been America's favorite pets. Despite the fact that dog training can be easy if you have some guidance, you still have to do the job. One way to make training simple is to get a breed that readily adapts to your lifestyle and that corresponds to what you want in a canine companion. Serious breeders will help you with this. They will tell you about their breed's inherent trainability—advice you should heed before making your final decision.

Rest assured that training does not strip a dog of natural instincts or *joie de vivre*. After all, these are the qualities that attract people to dogs in the first place. We want you to *celebrate* the canine spirit, not abuse it.

What training does, however, is structure the dog's responses, giving you a good *companion*. Training gives you an animal you can trust, even flaunt. In fact, it establishes a channel of communication between you and your dog that significantly enhances your mutual respect and friendship.

Akita. *Mary Bloom*

Australian Terrier. *Mary Bloom*

Chinese Cresteds. *Mary Bloom*

A dog can be trained effectively at any age. Often, the best results are achieved by working with young puppies. However, dogs are naturally adaptable and are usually eager to please. Consider the large number of grown dogs that change hands and how these dogs must learn the routines of their new homes. They do adapt, usually with great success.

Every civilized dog should know at least five basic commands: heel, sit, down, stay, and come. In formal dog training, these commands are first seen in The American Kennel Club's Canine Good Citizen® training, the introductory training program of The AKC. These basic commands also form the core of the exercises required for a Companion Dog (CD) title in American Kennel Club Novice

Obedience competition. Even if you don't take your dog beyond these beginning lessons, they are absolutely essential in making every dog a true companion.

Is My Breed Right for Training?

All dogs are suitable for training, although some breeds make naturally superior pupils because generations of ancestors were selected for trainability. Attend an Obedience event, or consult with owners, breeders, and AKC Standards for information about breeds that are readily trainable. If you purchase a breed not known for prowess in the Obedience ring, don't give up. Persevere. All dogs can learn and all breeds have been successful at obedience training. If training isn't going so well, maybe it's your training technique that's at fault. Your methods might be inconsistent or confusing. If you find you're at your wit's end, join a local obedience class, or contact a professional trainer for advice. Also, you may need to research training and behavior problems more thoroughly. There are hundreds of excellent books and videos on dog training. Many of these materials will cover training topics that range from basic training to advanced competitive obedience.

If you're wondering whether age is an obstacle, rest assured that there is no age limit for effective dog training. A dog is never too old or too young to begin training. You may have to be a little more persistent in training an adult dog, but there is no truth to the adage that "you can't teach an old dog new tricks." However, it is certainly easier if a foundation for learning is initiated right from the start of the relationship. When you're working with a puppy, remember that you should keep sessions very short, tasks should be easy, and your approach should be very positive and upbeat.

Working with a Dog's Instincts

One thing that all dogs have in common is a desire to please their owners. Unfortunately, an interspecies language barrier makes it difficult to get the point across. Training lets you overcome this barrier. Training establishes a means of communication between you and your dog that is guaranteed to brighten your relationship. After all, training shows your dog how to earn exactly what he craves—your approval.

Before you start actively training your dog, you might want to invest a little time learning a touch of the dog's language. We don't just mean barking. Body language is an extremely important communication tool between dogs and other creatures. If you spend just a few moments watching your dog, you may come away with the ability to understand, even "connect" with, your dog, much to his delight.

For instance, dogs often show they want to romp by making a "play bow." You'll recognize a play bow when your dog stretches out his forelegs before him and directs his rear end straight up on the air. Dogs instantly understand what this posture means, whether it is performed by another dog or a human being. Try imitating the play bow in front of your dog when he seems to be in the mood for fun. Chances are, your pet will reward you with an intriguing and exuberant response.

Other forms of canine body language worth understanding are signs of submission and aggression. Dogs who are submissive will often crouch down when you approach them, tuck their tail between their legs, or roll over to expose the belly. They may urinate on the floor. This dog doesn't want to assert himself. The dog may need a lot of reassurance. Training that includes plenty of praise may help the submissive dog "find itself."

An aggressive dog, besides showing teeth or letting out a low growl, may indicate aggression by raising the hair on the back, putting the ears forward, and holding the tail high. You can usually catch a glimpse of the dog's mood by the look in its eyes.

In fact, reading the expression in a dog's eyes is a powerful way to gauge his feelings, both good and bad. Most dogs do not like to maintain eye contact with a human being or a more dominant dog for long; they will shift their gaze sideways before looking back again. In the wild, animals often interpret direct staring as a challenge. Once you build a trusting relationship with your dog, you will probably find your dog sending long, loving looks your way without fear of reprisal.

Another point to remember before you begin the training process is that your puppy naturally begins to learn the moment he sets foot in your house, even if you do not know it. Dogs are creatures of habit. They soon establish routines and expectations based on what patterns are set by their owners. Consider the dog who perks up every time he hears a can opener pierce a can lid. Or the one who whines when he sees his owner pick up car keys because he has learned that soon enough he will be alone for the day. And surely you've seen many a dog surge into action by the sight or sound of a leash being picked up.

All of these are good examples of the power of consistency. Training is really the practice of consistently doing the same thing, in the same circumstances, over and over. Expose dogs enough times to predictable signals and they learn to respond accordingly. With obedience training, your goal is to direct this canine ability toward producing desirable behavior. But unlike the examples above, obedience training must be taught in relatively structured, regular sessions.

Black and Tan Coonhound. *Mary Bloom*

Eye contact is a potent control factor with any dog. In a sound, happy relationship, human/canine eye contact is more frequently the silent expression of mutual love.

Have confidence in your dog as you set out to train him, and your dog will show confidence in learning. This confidence is established by your consistently responding to a particular action with the same reaction. This means that certain actions (such as a puppy who bites you) are always prohibited, and certain others always encouraged. Inconsistency is the deadliest enemy of good training.

Identifying Your Training Philosophy

Dog training is a field with a very rich history. The American Kennel Club was founded in 1884, and the first formal Obedience trial was in 1933. From the 1940s to the 1960s, the general philosophy of dog training was that the dog must do what you tell him to do. Treats were not used during training, and physical corrections, such as a snap on the leash, were standard training practices.

In the 1980s, there was a shift in thinking for many dog trainers. Some expert trainers led seminars and produced books and videos advocating the use of positive training methods. These trainers advocated using food as a reward and means of motivating the dog during training. Some trainers began to borrow the technology used by marine mammal trainers. This technology involved using "clickers" as a conditioned reinforcer for the dog.

Today, there are several schools of thought regarding the best method for training dogs. Some instructors will tell you the most humane way to train the dog is with food. Others will tell you they prefer not to use food. You might observe one instructor who will tell you one type of collar is better; another instructor might tell you something that totally contradicts this. The bottom line in dog training is that in the hands of a competent person, most of the popular training strategies and techniques will result in success. The issue is that owners and instructors must choose the method best suited for themselves and their dogs.

One of the most important things you will do when you get ready to train your dog is to make some decisions about your own personal training philosophy. You will need to be a wise consumer, carefully evaluate all of your options, and choose the method and procedures that are best for you and your dog.

Rewards and Correction

A well-trained dog knows what he can and cannot do. This is only achieved by consistent reinforcement of desired behaviors. A dog who is praised when he does right and corrected when he does wrong will soon learn acceptable behavior. In training language, when an animal is rewarded for doing something right, it is called *positive reinforcement.* Positive reinforcement for dogs can be praise, hugs, pets, food or other treats, toys, and so on. *Corrections* in dog training range from a noise or words, indicating to the dog he is doing something wrong, to a quick snap of the leash. Corrections should be given in a fair, unemotional fashion. Striking, hitting, or kicking a dog is never appropriate during training.

Determining how you will reward your dog for good behavior will depend on the training philosophy you have selected. You might choose to use food as a reward. If you are training in a school that does not use food for training, reinforcement for your dog will come in the form of praise, hugs, and pets.

If you choose to use a specific technique like clicker training, you might not be very verbal during training sessions. However, when you are working with your dog without the clicker, you'll find the dogs are social creatures, and they love plenty of praise. Most dogs respond with joy to a simple "Good dog!" offered in your most supportive, warm voice. Others appreciate a nice pat on the head or neck. Whatever reinforcers you choose to use, your dog will let you know if he gets the message. The bottom line will be whether or not your training attempts are successful and you are meeting your goals.

When your dog does need to be corrected, remember that corrections are simply one more training technique, whether they are used in training sessions or when teaching the dog manners in the house. Many dog owners make a basic, destructive mistake of prolonging their displeasure with a dog who either violates the training or seems slow to learn. You must understand that dogs forget an event after a few minutes; they only know from your reaction that you are unhappy with them. You've got to catch a dog in the act of doing something wrong; if you don't, *forget about it.* Disciplinary action must be as closely connected with the misdeed as possible for positive results. Holding a grudge is destructive.

Always correct your dog without showing emotion. Remember that the ultimate goal, besides having a well-behaved pet, is to give your dog a chance to please you.

For example, let's look at how you might cope with the common problem of chewing. All puppies have a desire to chew on something, starting from the time they are quite young. It can be a real predicament when the puppy seems to prefer chewing on people or expensive furniture.

The most obvious way to approach this problem is to keep the puppy separated from things he should not chew whenever you cannot provide supervision. The puppy may need to be crated, for instance, or confined to a "safe" room like the kitchen.

But whenever the puppy is within sight and he takes something unacceptable into his mouth, like your clothing or hand, immediately correct him with a firm "No!" Offer the puppy an acceptable chew toy as an alternative. As soon as the puppy begins to chew on the acceptable toy, turn right around and praise on the spot: "Good dog!" The puppy thus learns that he will be corrected for doing something wrong, but will also receive abundant praise for doing something right.

In most cases, a sufficiently authoritative vocal correction makes the appropriate impression. When you are using corrections and they don't seem to be working, analyze the positive consequences you are giving the dog for the right behavior. Sometimes, more rewards for doing the right thing can be more helpful than corrections.

Newfoundland. *Mary Bloom*

Never strike your dog, with one possible exception. That exception is when a dog threatens to or is biting a person. In this case, you'll have to use your own judgment, based on your knowledge of your dog and of the circumstances surrounding the incident. If the use of physical force seems warranted, follow your instincts. Don't take any act of serious aggression anything less than seriously. Dogs who have shown any tendencies toward aggression absolutely require obedience training. Consult a veterinarian and trainer for advice in handling the aggressive dog.

While we're on the subject of praise and correction for aggressive behavior, never try to soothe or comfort a dog who is in the midst of lunging at other animals or people from the end of a leash. It will only reinforce this performance, because you would actually be praising the dog for acting like a monster. A better approach is to correct the dog, get him under control, and *then* praise acceptable behavior so he will associate praise with civil behavior.

Bichons Frise. *Mary Bloom*

A puppy has no concept of what he may or may not chew and, like a human infant, will put anything in reach in its mouth. When you catch your puppy chewing on an inappropriate item, remember that puppies need to chew to remove their deciduous teeth. Many owners will replace what a dog should not have with something that is acceptable for chewing.

We've said that it is not acceptable to hit your dog. When we say not to hit your dog, we mean using your hand, a newspaper, a stick, or anything else. You should also never threaten your dog. This is often the cause of "hand-shy" dogs who cringe at the sight of hands, upraised or not. The dog who expects a beating every time he sees an upraised hand has good reason to try to escape to safer ground.

There are some common mistakes that new dog owners make when it comes to teaching their dogs to be well-behaved family members. Somewhere along the way, someone started the technique of using a rolled-up newspaper to hit dogs who urinate in the house. We hope you will resist the temptation to use this "tool." If you think that the sound of the newspaper hitting the dog will frighten the dog into submission, consider this: Training does not occur by scaring a dog into making him do what you want and not do what you find objectionable.

Dogs want to please. When you have a persistent problem with your dog, such as a housebreaking problem, consider whether or not you are causing any part of this. Are you controlling the dog's meal times so that elimination is predictable? Are you getting up early enough to take your dog outside for adequate exercise before you go to work? If your dog is a young puppy, have you gone through all of the steps of crate training as a way to housebreak the dog?

Let's go over some basic guidelines for disciplining your dog. You've spent lots of time giving your dog adequate exercise, training, and play times so that he has appropriate activities. When your dog has done something wrong, you've observed the principle of immediate correction, waited for the dog to do what you want, and praised him for doing what's right. There's been no unpleasantness from you to the dog: no shouting, no hitting or violence, and no recriminations. You are treating your dog like you'd like to be treated. What more could a dog ask for?

First Lessons

Long before you begin teaching your dog the five basic obedience commands, you'll need to accomplish several small "training" tasks. They begin with housebreaking, of course, the first and most important lesson any dog must learn before he is an acceptable (and enduring) part of the family. Housebreaking is covered in the section "Crate Training" in Chapter 3.

In addition, during your first few weeks together, you should also begin to teach your puppy his name and how to walk on a leash. Some dogs do not take naturally to the restraint of a leash, so you will have to slowly and steadily familiarize your puppy to accept a light lead.

It's also wise to establish good habits right from the start so you won't have to fuss with a lot of troubleshooting later. This means keeping the puppy off the furniture, discouraging him from begging at the table, and preventing chewing, as well as other unacceptable practices. Let your puppy learn early what is acceptable and what is not.

Choosing the Right Instructor

Let's assume you have your new dog. You decide that you want to begin your training in the hands of an experienced trainer. To find an instructor, you can begin by observing training classes at your nearest AKC dog club. Another option for training is a private trainer or classes offered by a community agency such as a therapy dog group.

The best thing you can do when selecting a dog training class is to conduct observations of the instructor with a class of students and their dogs before you enroll in a particular class. If you are not permitted to come and observe, take it as a sign that you might not want to be in that class. Watch the methods the instructor is using and ask yourself whether you would be comfortable using those training procedures. Watch the dogs of some of the more advanced students as they work. Are these dogs trained as you would want your dog to be trained?

Talk to some of the students. Do they get one-on-one attention in the classes? Is the instruction individualized, with feedback given to each student as opposed to general comments to the whole class? Interview your instructor. Does this person have a credible track record when it comes to training? How many formal AKC Obedience (and other) titles has this instructor put on dogs? Are the students of this instructor earning titles? There are many trainers who are qualified to teach you how to teach your dog basic good manners. However, if you want to earn formal titles in areas such as Obedience, Agility, Tracking, or Field work, it will be hard for instructors to teach you to do this if they have not done it themselves. Does the instructor have a curriculum so you will know in advance what skills your dog will be learning? Is the instructor reinforcing, instructive, and encouraging with students? Is there a proper instructor- (and assistants-) to-student ratio? A great instructor can only do so much. If there is one instructor and 40 students (and their dogs) in a class, you could be in trouble. If the instructor has a dog who comes to class as a demo dog, watch the dog carefully. Is this a dog you would be proud to own? This dog is the product of the instructor's training.

If you have choices, don't make the mistake of selecting a dog training class based on its proximity to your home, cost, or the night of the week the class is held. Choose the class where you think you will find the most success as a learner. You owe this to your dog.

Types of Classes

If you decide to take your dog to a training class, there are several types of classes from which you can choose. If you have a puppy, you will enroll in a puppy class where you'll learn basic training and how to control your pup. There might be some lessons for *you* as a new puppy owner. These lessons might include grooming (such as how to trim your puppy's nails), crate training, nutrition, and so on.

If your dog is older, you can enroll in a Canine Good Citizen® (CGC) or beginning obedience class. In these classes, you'll learn to teach your dog basic skills such as heel, sit, down, stay, and come. Canine Good Citizen® classes also stress good manners for dogs. Your dog will learn to meet a friendly stranger, sit politely for petting, tolerate grooming by a stranger, and react appropriately in the presence of other dogs and distractions. Following CGC or beginning Obedience, you can move on to more advanced Obedience classes. In these classes, your dog will learn skills such as off-leash heeling, sit and down stays, and retrieving.

You may have a breed for which you'd prefer to start training with some special activity. For example, if you had a spaniel, a Sporting dog, you might have a local club that will teach you how to do Field work with birds. You might prefer starting your training with Field work rather than in formal Obedience classes. Or, if you have an athletic, fast dog, you might prefer to begin your training in an Agility class rather than in Obedience. All of these options are acceptable, but if you choose this route, remember that there aren't any shortcuts to a well-trained dog. Obedience training is the educational foundation a dog needs to excel in the other activities. If you choose to start your training in an area other than Obedience, you will still need to teach the basic skills of sit, down, stay, come, and heel.

Using a Training Collar and Lead

Serious, formal obedience training should be postponed until a dog is approximately six to eight months old. Prior to that age, dogs have little power of concentration, and intense lessons will only confuse them. As a rule of thumb, puppies who are still teething are too young for earnest instruction. However, even with puppies, classes can be beneficial and you can do short daily sessions to teach basic skills and good manners.

Before you begin training your dog, purchase a collar and lead (leash). This presents one of those philosophical choice points for you as an owner. There are several types of collars from which you can choose. The basic types of training collars include buckle collars and slip collars (which some people refer to as a "choke" collar). Some trainers use head collars or head halters, a collar that appears much like the halters worn by horses. These collars are suitable as training tools but are not permitted in AKC competitive events.

A slip collar is usually composed of metal links or nylon, with a metal ring at each end. It forms a loop when the collar is slipped through one of the rings. The other ring is used for attaching the leash. The correct collar size for a slip collar may be determined by measuring around the largest part of the dog's head and then adding one inch. Head collars include instructions for fitting or can be fitted when purchased. Buckle collars should be fitted so the dog cannot pull out of the collar, but not so tightly as to cause problems. Training leads are made of leather or webbing, generally a half inch to a full inch wide, and measure six feet in length. Once you have the collar and lead you'll be using, you should be ready to begin training.

Before you start actually training the dog, give him time to adjust to the new training collar by letting him wear it under supervision. After you feel the dog has accepted the collar, add the lead, take the handle, and walk around for a while, applying little or no pressure. Gradually increase your degree of control until the dog learns that even though the leash restrains him, there's no need to be afraid. Once you've reached the point where you can persuade your dog to come along in the general direction you want by gentle snaps on the lead (or using food as a lure if this is the method you choose), you are ready to begin obedience training.

Never use any type of training collar to exert constant pressure on the dog's neck. Any type of collar is abusive when used in an abusive fashion. In the right hands, training collars and leads are effective and humane tools. In the wrong hands, as with any other type of equipment that is misused, they can be harmful.

Class Time

Even if you go to class for an hour every week, training periods should take place regularly once or twice each day. Gradually increase the amount of time you spend training the dog from 15 to 30 minutes.

Longer sessions will not only tire the dog, but also tire the trainer, and overall training will suffer. Few things are worse for training than boredom, and that's exactly what is bound to happen when you try to pack too much learning into a session.

Be businesslike during training, but don't forget to be friendly (not frustrated) and offer your dog lavish praise. At the completion of each lesson, take time to play freely with your dog, easing the pressure and communicating the idea that there will be time for fun as well as work.

Heeling

The heeling exercise forms the foundation for all the obedience lessons to follow. Teaching a dog to heel is vital, if for no other reason than to enable you to walk him properly. It's a drag—literally—to walk a dog who pulls you every which way. A dog who will not walk on lead is simply not a good companion, but rather a nuisance. You shouldn't have to be a weight lifter to walk your dog and maintain control.

Before teaching heeling, you will have selected the training method you will use (or your instructor will have one that you will be using). For example, you might teach heeling using leash corrections, or you might teach heeling using a food lure for the dog. A lure is a piece of food that is held so that the dog follows it and gets in the correct position.

Using the method involving leash corrections to begin heeling, position the dog at your left side and start to walk while calling the dog's name and giving the command to heel: "Fido, heel!" A good training rule is to call the dog's name and then give the command for all movement exercises (heel, come) while giving only the command when you're teaching a motionless exercise (sit or stay).

Give the command just as you take the first step and, simultaneously, lightly snap the lead to persuade the dog to move along. Remember to step first with your left leg, the one closest to the dog if it's positioned correctly. (Another training rule: Step off with your right leg first if you're teaching a stationary exercise.)

Use only as much force as is necessary to get the dog moving with you. As you walk along, continue to urge the dog to walk at your left side, with the neck and shoulder approximately opposite and level with your left leg, by snapping the lead. Each time, give the command "Heel!" as you lightly snap. Each time you snap the leash and get the dog in position, use praise when he is in the correct position. Be realistic; it will take a good deal of work before the dog understands what he is meant to do, for this is the first time he has ever been asked to perform on command. If you are kind and patient and skillful, your dog will soon learn to do as asked—and without rancor, because he will realize that each time he responds properly, you are immediately pleased.

Using the second method (and there are several more from which you can choose), you'll have some food to use as a lure. Holding the food just in front of the dog's nose, say, "Fido, heel," as you move forward. The dog follows the food to get in the heel position. Practice heeling in brief, but lengthening, sessions, one or more times daily, until you have to give only one command as you start walking. Depending on the training method you've selected, you will no longer need to use the lead for correction, or you will be able to fade out the food. Practice moving in circles, around corners, and using other maneuvers, while keeping the dog at your side, until you are confident that your dog is walking with you of his own accord. When heeling is looking good, you are ready to move on to teaching the sit. While you go over each new exercise, don't forget to incorporate past assignments into your regimen in order to keep the lessons fresh.

Sit

The sit command, in obedience training, means that the dog should sit at the handler's left side, the dog's shoulder square to the handler's knee. The dog should sit facing straight ahead. In fact, truly well-trained dogs learn to heel by their handler's side and then to automatically sit as soon as motion is stopped, such as when coming to a street corner.

As with all other skills, there are several methods you can use to teach sit. One involves telling the dog to sit giving him some physical guidance. A second method involves using a food lure. A third method involves pushing the rear end of the dog into a sit as you give the command. Because the procedure can cause hip and joint problems, many trainers discourage the technique that involves pushing down on the dog's hips.

To teach your dog to sit by using physical guidance, start by heeling the dog at your side. When you stop, give the command, "Sit!" and place your left hand on the dog's back legs. "Tuck" the legs and guide the dog into a sitting position while your right hand uses the lead to hold the head up. Make the dog sit for a moment, then give the heel command and start walking once more. Again, stop, give the command to sit, guide the dog into position, and have him stay seated a little longer.

Using the procedure involving a food lure, stand in front of the dog. Hold a piece of food above the dog's nose. As you say, "Sit," move the food back over the dog's head. The dog will rock back into a sit to get the food. As soon as the dog sits, praise and give the food.

Gradually, as your dog catches on, you can fade the command, food, or the lead and hand guidance. With consistency and repetition, the dog will soon sit automatically when you come to a stop, and wait for you to either start moving again or give an established release command, such as, "Okay!"

Finally, when your dog has learned the full meaning of sit, and to sit when you stop walking, you are ready to teach the sit from any position. Concentrate on this phase, continuing the pure sit training until your dog will sit on command without the need for guidance or food. When this is accomplished, you can begin to introduce the stay command.

Stay

Once your dog understands the command to stay, she should remain in a seated position until you release her. It shouldn't matter if a cat passes by or a truckload of dog food jackknifes right in front of her. Your dog isn't completely trained unless her rear end maintains contact with the ground until the very moment you say it's okay to move.

To teach the stay command, place your dog in a sitting position at your left side while on the lead. Tell the dog to "Stay!" placing the palm of your left hand in front of the muzzle. As you say, "Stay!" pivot by stepping out on your right foot so that you are directly in front of the dog. You will now be facing the dog. Repeat the "Stay!" command in a coaxing but firm voice and keep your hands on the dog, if necessary, to reinforce the command.

During the first few attempts, don't try to make your dog stay for more than five or ten seconds before releasing her. Slowly increase the time and the distance you step away while cutting down on the repeated vocal commands, until your dog will stay on one command for at least three minutes.

It is important for you to understand that the properly trained dog will do what he is told the *first and only* time he is told. During training, it's okay to give as many commands as it takes to get the idea across, but you must reach the point where you need to say only one "heel," "sit," or "stay" for the dog to respond. Steer clear of the "rising voice syndrome." Most dogs aren't deaf, and they certainly aren't insensitive; they are often just improperly trained. Having to repeat your commands with ever-increasing volume and frustration will not produce an obedient animal. You should meet with success if you remain firm and unequivocal.

Down

To teach your dog to lie down on command, begin with the dog sitting at your side. As with the sit, there are several ways you can teach down. One method involves using some physical guidance and a second method, as with sit, involves using a food lure.

To teach down using physical guidance, kneel beside your dog. Reach over his back with your left arm, taking hold of his upper left front leg; take hold of his right front leg similarly with your right hand. Tell the dog "Down!" and put him gently into the down position by lifting the front feet off the ground and easing the body down until the dog is in a lying position. This way, there is no struggle between the two of you. Your dog is comforted by the fact that your arm is held securely around him and will not feel the urge to struggle against the pressure of a leash or hand by bracing his front legs.

When your dog is in the down position, release your grasp slowly, sliding your left hand around and leaving it on your dog's back. Keep saying "Down," as you do this. When the dog is in the down position, praise him and say, "Good, down." Make sure the dog remains in the down position for a few seconds, and then release and try again. Remember to keep training sessions short. If you use this method, you'll give the dog physical guidance in training until the dog goes down on command without you having to lift him, and he will stay quietly until released, without any pressure of your left hand on the back. After a few days, you should be able to stand straight up and only give one command "Down!" for your dog to lie at your side. Your goal is to improve your dog's down until he goes down when several feet away from you, still on lead.

Using the food lure technique to teach down, begin with the dog sitting at your left side. Bend over (or kneel beside the dog if he is small) with a piece of food in your right hand. As you say, "Down," move your hand downward from the dog's nose to the floor. The dog will start bending down to follow the food. When you get the food to the floor just in front of the dog's front paws, slide the food straight out in front of the dog. What you are doing here is moving the food in an L-pattern from the dog's nose to the floor, and then straight out in front of the dog. When the dog moves into the down position, give the food to the dog as you say, "Good, down."

When your dog has learned the down, start working on down-stay as you did with the sit. First, pivot out in front of the dog, praising the dog for down-stay. Back up a short distance, and then walk away only briefly. Finally, leave for longer periods until you can circle around your dog. You will find this exercise easier than the sit-stay lesson, because your dog already knows the meaning of "Stay!"

Come

Perhaps the most important basic command a dog must learn to respond to immediately is "Come!" Come is last on our list of training exercises because your dog should first know how to respond to the other commands we've covered.

While your dog is heeling at your side, take a sudden step back and say, "Fido, come!" As you give the command, snap the lead to make the dog turn around to her right while walking, and get her headed back toward you. When your dog is facing you, keep walking backward, urging her to come toward you with continued gentle snaps of the lead and repetitions of the "Come!" command.

If you have chosen to use food-training techniques, you will start walking and urge the dog to come to you as you back up and hold out some food and say, "Come."

Continue working on "Come" until the dog will come to you and sit in front of you. This is the beginning of combining some of the skills your dog has already learned. From here, your dog will also progress to a recall ("Come") from a sitting position at a distance. Notice that there is never a tug of war going on between you and your dog in teaching the dog to come on command. No matter which technique you use to train your dog to come when called, offering praise is especially important when the dog comes to you. You want your dog to learn that coming to you means good things will happen.

Irish Wolfhound. *Mary Bloom*

A beautiful, well-trained dog is a source of deep, lasting satisfaction. Owners who wish to spend time with their dogs can enter an exciting world of active competition, lifelong friendships, and a kind of pleasure that must be experienced to be fully appreciated.

▪ 6 ▪

COMPETITIONS FOR YOU AND YOUR DOG

W elcome to the world of AKC competitive events! In earlier chapters, you've read about the choices you make when you decide to get a dog, how to select and register your dog, the basics of puppy care, and how to teach your dog basic skills. We hope that, by now, you are enjoying your relationship with your new, canine family member. Now that your dog has settled into your home and you've been working on "home schooling," we'd like to encourage you to try a formal training class at an AKC club. Experienced trainers can teach you the tricks of the trade, and you'll find that you and your dog learn much faster when you don't have to figure out how to teach each skill on your own.

If your dog is of show quality, you can take advantage of AKC clubs across the country that offer classes to prepare you for competition and earning titles. Do you or your child have an interest in trying your hand at conformation dog shows? If so, Conformation or Junior Showmanship Competition could provide a wonderful new hobby for your family.

If for some reason you can't or don't want to show your dog in conformation, some of the programs in our Companion Events Department may appeal to you. Companion Events offers competition and titles that can be earned in Obedience, Agility, and Tracking. The Canine Good Citizen® Test, also a part of Companion Events, is an award rather than a title. For many dogs, the CGC award is the first AKC certificate earned. Each of the four areas in Companion Events serves to strengthen the bond between you and your dog through training and teamwork.

If you love the great outdoors and want to spend time having your dog do what he was bred to do, AKC Performance Events are for you.

Competitive Performance events include Coonhound events, Earthdog Tests, Field Trials and Hunting Tests, Herding, and Lure Coursing.

Conformation and Junior Showmanship

Showing dogs is an activity that can be enjoyed by just about everybody. Today's competitors come from all parts of the country and from all segments of society. Some people choose to show their own dogs, some have their dogs shown by friends, and others hire professional handlers whose expertise is exhibiting dogs to their best advantage.

The sport of showing dogs may confound a newcomer. In this section, you'll find a basic explanation of the dog show process for AKC conformation shows. If you then attend a few dog shows to observe the process in action—and sample the infectious appeal of seeing beautiful animals compete against one another for top honors—you, too, may join the growing number of dog show devotees.

Dog Shows: How They Work

Each year, more than 15,000 competitive events are held under American Kennel Club rules. There is a wide variety in the types of competition: Conformation, Field Trials, Hunting tests, Herding, Lure Coursing, Earthdog, Obedience, Tracking, Agility, and so on. In each of these categories, there are formal licensed events (point shows at which championship points or credit toward field or Obedience titles may be earned) and informal events (match shows at which no points or credits are earned). The majority of the competitive events held under AKC rules are *dog shows*, where the emphasis lies on *conformation*. After examining the entry, each judge decides how closely, in her opinion, the dogs measure up to that judge's mental image of the perfect dog as described in the breed Standard. The dogs are also compared to one another. Ultimately, the judge places the best dogs in each regular class from first to fourth.

Most dogs seen at shows are competing for points toward their championships. It takes 15 points to become a Champion of Record, which entitles the owner to use "Ch." before the dog's name. Essentially, these points are based upon the number of dogs in total competition—the more dogs, the more points. However, the number of dogs required for points varies with the breed, the sex, and the geographical location of the show in accordance with a schedule annually designated by The AKC to help equalize competition from breed to breed and area to area.

Saluki. *Mary Bloom*

Showing dogs is one of America's most popular participant sports and it keeps right on growing. In conformation competition, dogs are shown against one another and compared to their breed Standard by the judge in order to select the winners. Many rules govern the conduct of dog shows, but the attraction of the game is meeting the challenge of competition and coming up with the winner. The veteran exhibitor would have it no other way.

A dog can earn from 1 to 5 points at a show. Wins of 3, 4, or 5 points are termed "majors." The 15 points required for championship must be won under at least three different judges, and must include two majors won under different judges.

Dogs may compete in six or more regular classes to earn their points. These six classes are the Puppy (which may be divided by age), 12 to 18 month, Novice, Bred-by-Exhibitor, American-bred, and Open (which may also be divided for a number of reasons). The class in which the dog is entered depends, among other things, on its age and previous wins.

Only one male and one female of each breed can win points at each show. Only males compete against males, and females against females, in the classes for points.

The order of judging in every breed is the same. The judge begins with the Puppy class. In each class the dogs are evaluated, and the top four in the judge's opinion are placed first through fourth. However, only the first-place winner in each class remains in competition.

After the judge has made his or her decisions in the regular classes, the first-place winners from each class are brought back to compete against each other. This is called the Winners Class. The dog selected best is the Winners Dog. He is the male who receives the points at the show.

Following selection of the Winners Dog, the dog that placed second to him in his original class of competition is brought into the ring to compete with the other class winners for Reserve Winners Dog. The Reserve will receive the points if for any reason the Winners win is disallowed by The AKC.

The same process is repeated for bitches, with a Winners Bitch (the only female of the breed to receive points at the show) and a Reserve Winners Bitch being selected.

The judge must now evaluate one more class in the breed and make three more awards. The Best of Breed Competition class includes all the Champions of Records competing, male and female, and the Winners Dog and Winners Bitch. The judge reviews all the dogs and selects one Best of Breed. Then, between the Winners Dog and Winners Bitch, the judge selects a Best of Winners. If either the Winners Dog or Winners Bitch is selected Best of Breed, the dog automatically becomes Best of Winners. The judge then finishes the breed judging by selecting a Best of Opposite Sex to the Best of Breed.

At an all-breed show (a show where all AKC breeds can enter), this process of elimination takes place in all the breeds represented. Then, each Best of Breed winner competes for first place within its Group. Four placements are awarded in each Group, but only the first is eligible to compete in the final competition. This whittles the competition down to seven individuals vying for Best in Show. At the largest all-breed events, nearly 4,000 contestants are evaluated before one dog is awarded the Best in Show ribbon.

Labrador Retriever. *Mary Bloom*

Manchester Terriers. *Mary Bloom*

To the dog exhibitor, every new puppy is a new beginning and every promising puppy generates the hope of winning days ahead. The beautiful new puppy also means training, grooming, and long hours of work, but it's worth everything when the puppy you banked on justifies your faith. There are sessions where the puppy will learn to allow itself to be handled: to have its mouth closely examined, to gait in a straight line on a loose lead, and to have its rear parts handled without protesting. These are the early lessons for every potential show dog.

Smooth Collie. *Mary Bloom*

Confused? This may all be a little overwhelming at first, like learning a new language. Rest assured that it becomes much clearer after you've sat through the actual process a few times. The other bonus of attending dog shows is the chance to mingle with a large crowd of enthusiastic experts, just waiting to interpret the proceedings as they unfold. Ask away.

Junior Showmanship. Junior Showmanship is the activity that teaches young people how to show dogs, develop good sportsmanship, and learn about dogs and dog shows. For youngsters between the ages of 10 and 18, an entire class of competition exists to help develop handling skills. Junior Showmanship competition is judged solely on the ability and skills of the handler—not on the dog's actual conformation. Junior Showmanship is a great place to learn skillful dog handling for conformation competition. It's also a terrific way to become acquainted with other young people who share an interest in showing dogs.

The best way for a young person to get involved in showing dogs is to watch a Junior Showmanship class at a dog show. Many local AKC clubs welcome young members to their training classes for conformation and other AKC activities.

Companion Events: Obedience, Agility, Tracking, and Canine Good Citizen

Obedience Trials

The purpose of formal obedience competitions is to demonstrate the usefulness of the dogs as companions. In competitive obedience trials, a dog's ability to perform a prescribed set of exercises is tested. A judge scores the performance for each exercise. Conformation has no bearing on the dog's ability to compete in Obedience; individuals who would be disqualified from the show ring, such as dogs who are spayed or neutered, may compete for an Obedience title.

Obedience is divided into three levels: Novice, Open, and Utility. At each level, competitors work for an AKC Obedience title. There are also non-regular Obedience classes, which are considered fun or practice classes. These classes do not result in the dog earning a title. Rally Obedience is the latest addition to the non-regular classes.

Basenji. *The AKC*

Novice. The first level of formal obedience competition is Novice. The Novice exercises include those things all dogs should be taught to make them good companions. The exercises in the Novice Obedience class are Heeling on Lead and Figure 8, Stand for Exam, Heel Free (off-lead), Recall, Long Sit (one minute), and Long Down (three minutes). Successful competitors in the Novice class earn the title of Companion Dog (CD).

Open. Open work follows the Novice class. Some people think of this as the Master's degree for dogs. Open Obedience exercises include Heel Free and Figure 8, Drop on Recall, Retrieve on Flat, Retrieve over High Jump, Broad Jump, Long Sit (three minutes), and Long Down (five minutes). To compete in Open Obedience, a dog must have earned the Novice title. When the dog completes an Open title, it is called a Companion Dog Excellent (CDX). If you think back to titles and awards the dog earned before Open competition, Canine Good Citizen training (and testing) was all done on-lead. As the dog progressed to Novice competition, many of the exercises were on-lead, but off-leash work was introduced. The distinction between Novice and Open is that in Open, as soon as the handler enters the ring, the steward takes the leash. Each and every routine is done off-lead. It is during Open competition that handlers really begin to hope they have spent enough time training their dogs.

Utility. The third and most advanced level of formal Obedience is Utility. The Utility exercises include Signal Exercise, Scent Discrimination, Directed Retrieve, Moving Stand and Examination, and Directed Jumping. To compete in Utility, the dog must have earned the CDX title. The title earned by dogs mastering Utility work is Utility Dog (UD); beyond the UD is UDX (Utility Dog Excellent). Dogs who have earned the Utility Dog title can work toward an Obedience Trial Championship (OTCH), the ultimate distinction.

To earn an Obedience title in any of the three classes, a dog must earn three "legs." To earn a qualifying leg, a dog must score at least 170 points out of a possible 200, and earn more than 50 percent on each exercise.

There are AKC Obedience clubs all over the country and these clubs can provide you with training for Obedience competition. Training enhances the bond between an owner and dog. Obedience training, in particular, provides a solid foundation for all other actions in the sport of dogs. Experienced trainers will tell you that Obedience-trained dogs are the honor roll students when they participate in other performance activities.

Rally Obedience. In these classes, the team of dog and handler move continuously and perform the exercises indicated by a sign at each location. After the judge's "forward" command, the team is on its own to complete the entire sequence correctly. Unlimited communication from the handler to the dog between signs is to be encouraged and not penalized. Handlers are permitted to talk, praise, encourage, clap their hands, pat their legs, or use any verbal means of encouragement. However, handlers may not touch their dog or make corrections.

Agility

It is only fitting that Agility, a fast-paced, take-your-breath-away event, is one of the fastest growing AKC programs. Agility is the sport for handlers and dogs who want to do something athletic. There is nothing slow and leisurely about Agility, although enthusiastic participants rave about the sense of well-being that comes from the rigorous exercise involved with the sport.

Agility is the competitive event where a dog demonstrates her ability to be steady and under good control, yet fast and agile as she proceeds with her handler through an obstacle course. In Agility, handlers and dogs run as fast as they can with the goal of doing well in both speed and accuracy. Agility is a spectator sport as well. When Agility is at a show, you can bet the stands will be full and the fans will be cheering and screaming for every dog and handler.

Agility dogs are athletes; the sport is very physical and proper training for both dogs and handlers is required. Agility obstacles include the open tunnel, closed tunnel, pause table, weave poles, dog walk, seesaw, tire jump, broad jump, jumps (bar, panel, and so on), and A-frame. Let's take a look at what your dog would have to do in Agility for each of the obstacles.

Open tunnel. Because the open tunnel is one of the easiest agility obstacles to learn, many trainers teach this obstacle first. In an Agility course, the dog runs to one end of the tunnel, enters, and exits the other end.

Closed tunnel. The closed tunnel is a fabric tunnel with one end collapsed. The dog runs to the tunnel's open end, enters, pushes through the tunnel, and exits the closed end.

Tire jump. The tire jump obstacle is suspended from a frame. This is the one obstacle that the dog must jump through, rather than over. The dog approaches the tire and jumps through the opening.

Weave poles. Weave poles are thought by many to be the most fun to watch and the most difficult to train. In the weave pole obstacle, dogs approach and enter a series of 6 to 12 poles at top speed. The dog weaves through each pole quickly, slalom-style, and exits at the last pole.

Jumps. Agility jump obstacles involve the dog jumping over a bar, panel, and double or triple jump. The jump height for each dog is based on the dog's height. Dogs are measured and Agility handlers are given an Agility jump-height card that specifies the dog's proper jump heights.

Broad jump. The broad jump is a series of raised boards. In this obstacle, the dog jumps over the broad jump a distance that is twice the dog's jump height.

Dog walk. The dog walk, A-frame, and seesaw are called "contact obstacles" in Agility. These obstacles must be performed in a safe manner and the dog must break from a full-speed run to a slower pace and touch the "contact zones" at each end of the boards.

For the dog walk, the dog goes up an angled plank that has a contact zone of 42 inches that must be touched by the dog. The dog then crosses the top plank, which is raised and parallel with the ground, and runs to the bottom, touching the "downside" contact zone on the plank.

A-frame. In the A-frame obstacle, the dog scales up an A-frame, climbs quickly over the top, and runs to the bottom, touching the contact zone.

Seesaw. The seesaw obstacle looks similar to the seesaws designed for children. The dog runs up to the seesaw and must touch the "upside" contact zone before moving quickly to the middle and then exiting after touching the "downside" contact zone on the plank, not exiting until the plank has touched the ground.

Pause table. The pause table demonstrates control by the handler. While the dog is running at full speed, the handler must be able to stop the dog for five seconds. The dog approaches the table, leaps onto it, and follows the handler's instructions to down or sit. The dog is required to stay in position for five seconds and then leaves the table when commanded by the handler. The pause table is the only obstacle that demonstrates control; the contact obstacles are meant for safety during a dog's high-speed performance.

In AKC Agility, there are five different height categories so that each dog can compete against dogs of her own size. Agility has several different titles; in some of the classes, you'll notice the contact (slow down) obstacles have been deleted. These are the classes for the handlers who want action that is fast, fast, fast.

In Agility, the titles dogs can earn range from Novice to Excellent. Beyond Excellent, there are national championships and the coveted Agility MACH title, which stands for Master Agility Champion.

Tracking Tests

You've seen the movies with the handlers and their dogs trudging through thick swampland to find somebody. You may also have read about your local police bringing out the K-9 unit dogs when a suspect is on the run. These well-trained canines are tracking dogs.

AKC Tracking Tests demonstrate the dog's ability to track and follow human scent. The tests simulate the skills a dog would need to find a child lost in the woods or a person who had run across a parking lot.

Tracking Dog (TD). The beginning Tracking title is the TD, or Tracking Dog title. To earn a TD, a dog must follow a track 440 to 500 yards long with three to five changes of direction. Each track is allowed to age for 30 minutes to two hours before the dog begins the test. An article is left at the end of the track by the person who lays the track and the dog must find it to successfully pass the test. During a Tracking test, the handler follows the dog on a long tracking line (leash).

Tracking Dog Excellent (TDX). The TDX builds on the skills the dog has learned while completing the TD. To pass the TDX test, the dog must complete a track that is three to five hours old. Distance is increased for the TDX and in this test, the dog must complete a track 800 to 1,000 yards with five to seven changes of direction. The TDX track also includes cross tracks, which means a person crosses the original track, thereby making the dog's job more complex.

Variable Surface Tracking (VST). The VST title is the newest addition to The AKC's tracking program. VST is designed for a realistic, modern world where many dog owners live in cities and the skills of tracking dogs are needed. In VST, dogs track through urban settings. The VST track is three to five hours old and the track is run on *variable surfaces*. A typical VST test track might require the dog to track on a city street, through a parking lot, around a building, and into a field.

Champion Tracker (CT). A dog who earns all three Tracking titles (TD, TDX, and VST) earns the prestigious title of Champion Tracker.

Tracking is an activity that you and your dog can do together. You'll both enjoy being outside and you will experience the thrill of watching your dog use his amazing scenting abilities.

Canine Good Citizen® Test

The AKC Canine Good Citizen® (CGC) Program is a two-part program designed to teach responsible dog ownership to owners and basic good manners to dogs. The foundation for the program is the ten-step CGC test that includes the following items:

1. Accepts a friendly stranger
2. Sits politely for petting
3. Appearance and grooming
4. Out for a walk (on a loose lead)
5. Walking through a crowd
6. Sit and Down on command and Stay in Place
7. Coming when called
8. Reaction to another dog
9. Reaction to distractions
10. Supervised separation

Canine Good Citizen training is considered by many to be a good starting point for any other formal training. In the hands of a good instructor, you and your dog can get ready for the CGC Test in eight to ten weeks if you go to class one hour per week and practice 15 minutes each day.

Because the CGC Test is not always administered by licensed AKC judges, Canine Good Citizen is an award program as opposed to an official title. Don't underestimate the value of this award, however. Some communities give reductions in licensing to CGC dogs, there are CGC apartment buildings where CGC dogs are welcome, and 15 states and the United States Senate have CGC resolutions. The Canine Good Citizen Test is used by some therapy dog groups as a key component of the evaluation for potential therapy dogs.

The CGC Test is administered on-lead and all dogs who pass the test, including purebred and mixed breed dogs, receive a certificate from The American Kennel Club. AKC clubs can give the test as well as veterinarians, vet techs, private trainers, and other canine professionals. Dogs of all ages can take the CGC Test. There is nothing more heartwarming than watching a 15-year-old senior dog earn the CGC award.

Performance Events

Coonhound Tests

There is no limit to the fun offered to the six purebred Coonhounds. Treeing Walkers, Black and Tans, Plotts, English, Blueticks, and Redbones all participate in Bench shows, Field Trials, Nite Hunts, and Water Races. Many of the Coonhound events test the dog's ability to follow the scent of raccoons and signal to a handler that the quarry has been treed. The Coonhounds have their own annual National Championship.

Earthdog Tests

Earthdog Trials are for dogs who "go to ground." Think back to what certain breeds have been bred to do. Smaller terriers and Dachshunds were originally bred to go into dens or dirt tunnels after quarry. You might have noticed that the shape of some of the breeds is perfectly designed to fit into the long narrow hole dug by a badger.

Dachshunds, Australian Terriers, Bedlington Terriers, Border Terriers, Cairn Terriers, Dandie Dinmont Terriers, Fox Terriers, Jack Russell Terriers, Lakeland Terriers, Manchester Terriers, Miniature Bull Terriers, Miniature Schnauzers, Norfolk Terriers, Norwich Terriers, Scottish Terriers, Sealyham Terriers, Skye Terriers, Welsh Terriers, West Highland White Terriers, and Silky Terriers are all breeds that can take part in Earthdog events.

There are four levels of Earthdog. Introduction to Quarry is for beginning handlers and dogs, and if you're just getting started, it would be good for you. Once you've had some experience, you can advance to Junior Earthdog, Senior Earthdog, and Master Earthdog.

Field Trials and Hunting Tests

Field Trials are held separately for pointing breeds, retrievers, and spaniels, as well as Beagles, Basset Hounds, and Dachshunds. Field Trials are practical demonstrations of the dogs' ability to perform, in the field, the functions for which they were bred. The titles that are awarded are Field Champion (FC) and Amateur Field Champion.

Both Field Trials and Coursing offer a National Field Champion or National Amateur Field Champion title each year. This is the most coveted title in Performance Events.

Retrievers, pointing breeds, and spaniels are also eligible to participate in Hunting Tests. Here, owners of these breeds can obtain an evaluation of their dogs' hunting ability. A dog's performance is evaluated at three levels, and again, each succeeding level is increasingly difficult. Dogs successfully completing the respective levels earn the titles Junior Hunter, Senior Hunter, and Master Hunter. The variety of events in fieldwork reflects each breed's original function.

Beagles. For more than 105 years, dog fanciers have been competing in Beagle Field Trials. Beagles work in one of three different formats, which include Small Pack, Large Pack, and Brace.

Beagle. *Mary Bloom*

Basset Hounds and Dachshunds. The events for Bassets and Dachshunds are similar to Beagle Brace Trials. For these breeds, there are Field Trials but no Hunting Tests.

Pointing breeds. Brittanys, English Setters, German Shorthaired Pointers, German Wirehaired Pointers, Pointers, Gordon Setters, Irish Setters, Vizslas, Weimaraners, and Wirehaired Pointing Griffons can participate in Pointing Breed Field Trials and Hunting Tests. The pointing breeds are tested on their ability to find birds, point, and retrieve. The AKC has offered Pointing Breed Field Trials for more than 72 years.

Retrievers. Retrievers retrieve game. In retriever events, dogs are tested on their ability to mark the location of game and deliver it to their handlers. Both Hunting Tests and Field Trials for Retrievers range from beginning levels to more difficult. At the more difficult levels of Retriever work, dogs have to do "blind retrieves." The following retrievers participate in Retriever events: Chesapeake, Curly-Coated, Flat-Coated, Golden, and Labrador Retrievers.

Standard Poodles also compete in Retriever Hunts Tests, and although it has "spaniel" in its name, the Irish Water Spaniel competes in Retriever events.

Spaniels. The key feature of field work for spaniels is that spaniels are required to flush game. In Field Trials and Hunting Tests, spaniels are judged on their ability to hunt, flush, and retrieve game on both land and in water. Spaniels participating in Hunting Tests include: Clumber, Cocker, English Cocker, English Springer, Field, Sussex, and Welsh Springer Spaniels. Cocker, English Cocker, and English Springer Spaniels may also compete in Field Trials.

Wirehaired Dachshund. *Mary Bloom*

Pointer. *The AKC*

Field Trials for pointing breeds, retrievers, and spaniels, along with events for Beagles, Basset Hounds, and Dachshunds, enjoy a large, enthusiastic following in the United States. These events serve to keep the breed's aptitude for their original work sharp while providing exciting recreation for large numbers of people.

Herding

If you own a herding breed, consider giving your dog a chance to try herding. A dog's ability to herd is the result of centuries of breeding, and watching a herding dog work is a thrill to behold.

AKC Herding events are open to all herding breeds, plus Rottweilers and Samoyeds. In Herding Tests, dogs are judged against a set of performance standards. In Herding Trials, dogs compete against the standard and each other for placements and prizes. Stock used at Herding Trials can include ducks, cattle, goats, or sheep. To find out if you and your dog would enjoy herding, you might attend a herding clinic or herding instinct test. These activities are given by AKC clubs throughout the year.

The Herding program is divided into Testing and Trial sections. In the Testing section, dogs can earn the titles of Herding Test Dog (HT) and Pre-Trial Tested Dog (PT). The former is awarded to dogs who show an inherent herding ability and are trainable in herding. The PT title, on the other hand, is earned by dogs with some training in herding who can, therefore, herd a small group of livestock through a simple course.

Trials offer four titles, beginning with Herding Started (HS), Herding Intermediate (HI), and Herding Excellent (HX) titles. After earning an HX, dogs can then accumulate the necessary 15 championship points for the Herding Championship (HC). Such a dog is proficient in herding and capable of controlling even the most difficult livestock in diverse situations. The trials are run on three distinct courses, which differ in both the physical aspects and style of herding.

Australian Shepherd. *Mary Bloom*

Herding Tests and Trials are a fairly recent addition to The AKC events in which dogs can distinguish themselves. It is truly amazing how many dogs of the herding breeds demonstrate their proficiency even if they have never been in the presence of livestock.

Lure Coursing

If you are the proud owner of a sighthound, a dog that can run like the wind, Lure Coursing might just be an activity you'd like to try with your dog. In Lure Coursing, dogs follow an artificial lure around a course on an open field. The lure is moved mechanically and the speed can be easily controlled.

Breeds that compete in Lure Coursing include Afghan Hounds, Basenjis, Borzois, Greyhounds, Ibizan Hounds, Irish Wolfhounds, Italian Greyhounds, Pharaoh Hounds, Rhodesian Ridgebacks, Salukis, Scottish Deerhounds, and Whippets.

Lure Coursing dogs are judged on speed, enthusiasm, agility, endurance, and their ability to follow the lure.

Whatever your interest and wherever you live, it shouldn't be difficult to locate an AKC competitive event in your area. A list of upcoming shows and trials is included with each issue of the AKC's monthly magazine, *AKC Gazette*. Many clubs advertise their events in local newspapers as well.

Jack Russell Terrier. *Mary Bloom*

To a dedicated breeder, consistency of type in his dogs is a great satisfaction. Always remember, though, that breeding dogs should never be undertaken lightly or for the wrong reasons. If you plan to breed your dog, you must assume responsibility for the health and safety of the mother and puppies. Otherwise, if you don't plan to show, have your dog neutered. You won't be sorry.

• 7 •

BREEDING

We can't say it often enough. If you have a dog who is a pet and who you are not going to show, you should have your dog spayed or neutered. We believe that the breeding of purebred dogs should be left to knowledgeable, responsible breeders. These breeders are involved in their national breed clubs; they go to the national specialty shows for the breed; they are well-versed in the genetic problems that can occur in the breed; they have obtained championships on their dogs; and they have an organized breeding plan designed to contribute to or improve the breed.

Having said this, it may be that you plan to take all of the right steps before breeding your dog. You may be thinking now that you may *eventually* decide to breed your dog. For this reason, we'd like to provide you with some general information on canine reproduction.

If you are thinking of breeding your dog in the future, please don't take the responsibility lightly. If you are going to breed your dog, you must have plans for each and every puppy before the litter is even conceived. This is the mark of a responsible breeder.

Also, it is overly optimistic to assume that you can recoup your investment or make a profit by breeding dogs. Few people come out ahead by selling puppies. After they have paid stud fees, provided veterinary care and food for the mother and litter, and have accounted for their enormous investment of time, little profit is left.

Breeding dogs also carries emotional costs. Ask a breeder what it's like to see a bitch through a difficult birth or Caesarean section, or to witness the death of a beloved bitch or one of her puppies. Death plays as large a role as life when it comes to breeding dogs.

If you decide to go forward and become a breeder, we hope you will embrace the belief that each new litter you produce should represent an improvement over the last. This means that you don't choose the dog that lives down the street to breed with your bitch because he happens to be close by and no stud fee is involved. You should start with show-quality dogs. You'll want to be in touch with known, reputable breeders of your breed so they can help you find an individual dog whose bloodlines will strengthen your dog's weaknesses and emphasize your dog's good qualities. The rewards of your discretion will be long-lived.

Selecting Breeding Partners

It is not our purpose here to delve into the genetics of breeding better dogs. There are many excellent books entirely devoted to the genetics of the dog and how to breed. However, we wish to make three important points concerning the selection of a breeding partner for your dog.

First, as complicated as genetics may seem, there is a simple principle to bear in mind in selecting dogs: Namely, you breed animals who complement one another. This means, for example, if your dog's coat is not as good as it might be, locate a partner with a good coat from a line with good coats. The truth is, of course, that selecting breeding partners is more complex because you must weigh all the factors that make up the two animals. Obviously, this is one area where experienced breeders are your absolute best source.

Border Terrier. *The AKC*

Correct temperament is one of the breeder's most pressing priorities. Even though most dogs will never see the inside of a show ring, the way they respond and relate to people is directly tied to how well they conform to the Standard. A person who wants a good companion dog should never be forced to choose between bad temperament and beauty.

The second and third points we want you to digest boil down to two words: *temperament* and *health*. Temperament is a hereditary trait in dogs. Selection over many generations eventually produced breeds with the correct temperament to pull sleds, follow scent on trails, or retrieve game. The inheritance factors of temperament are complex. However, never consider breeding a dog with questionable temperament. You impose a major disservice on both human and canine communities if you produce another generation of skittish or bad-tempered animals.

In addition, dogs are subject to many hereditary defects, some of which are potentially crippling or fatal. If you breed, you carry the responsibility of ensuring that the dogs you produce are not affected by the major known hereditary diseases occurring in your breed. Both your dog's breeder and your veterinarian can advise you. Please do not take this warning lightly. Consider how devastated you would feel if the beautiful eight-week-old puppy you place in a loving home develops a crippling hip problem at one year of age. Ignorance is no excuse for having contributed to this tragic situation.

Reproductive Physiology

The age at which dogs reach sexual maturity depends to a large extent on their breed. Small breeds tend to mature faster than large breeds. In general, male puppies become fertile after 6 months of age and reach full fertility by 12 to 15 months. Healthy stud dogs may remain sexually active and fertile up to eight or ten years old or older. Adult males are able to mate at any time.

Bitches experience their first *estrus* (also known as *season* and *heat*) sometime after 6 months of age, although a wide variation occurs, with 18 months not uncommon in some larger breeds. Estrus recurs at intervals of 6 to 7 months on the average, depending on the breed and individual, until late in life. During the estrus period, the female is fertile and will accept the male.

The reproductive cycle of the bitch is divided into four stages:

1. *Proestrus.* This is the time when males are attracted to females. A bloody vaginal discharge is observed, as well as distinct swelling of the external genitalia. Proestrus lasts approximately nine days; the female, however, will not allow mating at this stage.

2. *Estrus.* Estrus also lasts approximately nine days. During this phase, females will allow males to mount. Ovulation usually occurs in the first 48 hours; however, this is extremely variable. Fertilization can take place during estrus if the bitch is inseminated by a fertile dog.

3. *Diestrus*: This third stage, lasting 60 to 90 days, occurs when the reproductive tract is under the control of progesterone. This happens whether or not the bitch becomes pregnant. False pregnancy, a condition in which the bitch shows all the symptoms of being pregnant although she has not conceived, is occasionally seen during diestrus.

4. *Anestrus*: This is the period following diestrus when no sexual activity takes place. It lasts for three to four months.

Breeding

There are many schools of thought regarding when to begin breeding a bitch. It is customary, however, not to breed at the first heat to avoid imposing the stress of pregnancy and lactation on a young, growing animal. Another common practice is to avoid breeding a bitch on consecutive heats, to allow sufficient time for recuperation between pregnancies. If breeding on the first heat or on consecutive heats occurs, extra attention and care are mandatory to reduce the risk of potential problems. Ask your veterinarian for advice on this subject.

The bitch should be in good condition. This means, most emphatically, that she is not overweight, and is in good muscle tone. She should have a thorough prebreeding physical examination by a veterinarian. Her vaccinations should be current, and she should be tested and treated for parasites. You may wish to have her tested for brucellosis, a bacterial disease that can cause sterility or spontaneous abortion in affected dogs. (Ask the owner of the stud dog if he's had his dog tested for brucellosis, since a male carrier can infect the female. If he is used for breeding frequently, a test before each mating is probably impractical. In that case, it is usually acceptable for the dog to be kept away from pregnant, whelping, and nursing bitches, and to be tested twice yearly.)

Breeding management varies widely from breed to breed. Most commonly, the breeding takes place between the tenth and fourteenth days after the onset of proestrus. The signs of estrus are obvious in some bitches, but others benefit from having vaginal smears analyzed by a veterinarian to identify the fertile period. While the bitch will stand for the male, mating every other day for a total of two or three times is considered good breeding management for both dogs.

Females are usually less inhibited by new environments, so bitches are commonly taken to the stud. The first time a young male is used, breeding will proceed more smoothly if an experienced bitch is used. Nevertheless, sometimes breeding must be assisted by humans, to provide support or guidance. Some breeds are more apt to need assistance than others because of anatomical considerations. This is another area that should be discussed with your own dog's breeder prior to the actual breeding.

During breeding, the male will mount the female from the rear and clasp her middle with his front legs. He will then rapidly thrust his pelvis until he penetrates the bitch and ejaculation takes place. After his pelvic thrusts cease, the dogs remain locked together by a normal swelling that takes place in the male's penis. This is commonly called a *tie,* and may be expected to last from 10 to 30 minutes. Do not try to separate the dogs during the tie, because it can injure them. The male may turn around while he and the female are joined, so that they stand rear to rear. At the end of the tie, the dogs will separate naturally.

Artificial insemination in dogs is approved by The American Kennel Club. For complete details about AKC policies, contact Registration Service, 5580 Centerview Drive, Raleigh, NC 27606.

Pregnancy

A normal canine pregnancy lasts approximately 63 days following conception. Signs of pregnancy include increased appetite, weight, and breast size; however, bitches with false pregnancy can also exhibit these symptoms. Veterinarians can usually diagnose pregnancy thorough abdominal palpation at 28 days or by using ultrasound or x-ray tests.

Once pregnancy is confirmed, it's time to review special feeding requirements and what to expect before, during, and after the birth with your veterinarian. You should also be briefed on how to recognize and respond to an emergency.

A few days before she gives birth (known as *whelping*), the bitch may refuse to eat and start to build her nest, where she plans to have her puppies. Unless you introduce her beforehand to a whelping box, the delivery room may be your closet, the space under your bed, or any number of places you would probably consider inappropriate.

A whelping box should be sufficiently large to accommodate a comfortable stretch for the bitch. It should have low sides and be placed in a warm, dry, draft-free, and secluded place. Place towels or other soft material in the bottom of the whelping box. Fresh newspapers are also fine, as they may be easily removed and replaced as they become soiled during whelping. Once whelping is completed, however, you should replace the newspapers with something that provides better footing for the puppies.

Shortly before whelping, the bitch's body temperature will drop to 99 degrees or lower (normal temperature for a dog is between 100 and

102.5 degrees). By this time, you should have shaved her belly, where appropriate, to allow the puppies to find the nipples. If she has a long or dense coat, you should also shave and clean the area around her genitals.

Around 24 hours after her temperature drops, she can be expected to enter the first stage of labor, when the cervix dilates and opens the birth canal for the passage of puppies. At this time, she will pant, strain, appear restless, or may vomit. Vomiting is normal at the onset of labor, but persistent vomiting may be a sign of illness. This stage of labor is followed by actual abdominal straining and production of the puppies and placentas.

Birth

Most bitches give birth easily, without the need of human help. Each puppy emerges in its own placental membrane, which must be removed before the puppy can breathe. The mother usually takes care of this by tearing off and eating the membrane, and then severing the umbilical cord. After delivery, she will lick each puppy to stimulate his or her breathing. Frequent licking, which continues for three weeks or so, also has another vital function: It stimulates the puppy to excrete waste. Without maternal assistance puppies cannot do so. At the time of birth, new mothers are also busy cleaning their offspring, warming them, and allowing them to suckle. It is very important for the puppies to suckle soon after emerging from the womb. Suckling lets them ingest colostrum, a milklike substance containing maternal antibodies that is produced in the mammary glands just after birth. Colostrum helps the newborn puppies fight infection in their early days, while their own immune systems mature.

A placenta follows each puppy after a few minutes and is generally eaten by the mother. Try to keep track of the number of placentas delivered to make sure one is produced for each puppy. A retained placenta may cause infection.

Occasionally, a bitch neglects to remove a placental membrane or sever an umbilical cord, or she may be unable to do the job herself. In that case, you must handle the situation without delay. Puppies can remain inside the placental sac after birth for only a few minutes before the oxygen supply is depleted. Remove the puppy from the sac by tearing the membrane first from the face and head and then working backward. Then clean any mucus or fluid from the puppy's mouth and nose, and stimulate its circulation by rubbing it briskly with a towel. Tie off the umbilical cord with unwaxed dental floss, and cut the cord about two inches from the abdomen. Apply iodine to the cut end to prevent a navel infection.

When to Call the Veterinarian

If events during delivery take an ominous turn, don't hesitate to call the veterinarian for assistance. Abnormal conditions that signify trouble include

- indications of extreme pain
- straining labor for more than three hours without passing a puppy, whether one or no puppies have been delivered previously
- trembling, shivering, or collapse
- passage of a dark green or bloody fluid before the birth of the first puppy (after the first puppy, this is normal)

Also, veterinarians commonly recommend that you schedule a health check for the bitch and her puppies within a day of the delivery.

Newborn Puppies

Newborn puppies are unable to control their body temperature. They must be kept in a place where the temperature is approximately 85 degrees Fahrenheit. Chilling during these early days of life causes stress and predisposes the puppies to infectious disease. The puppies' environment may be kept warm by using a well-insulated heating pad (preferably one that uses circulating warm water), an electric heating bulb, or a hot water bottle covered with a towel for protection.

Saint Bernard. *Mary Bloom*

Finnish Spitz. *The AKC*

Sometimes a bitch is unable or unwilling to care for her puppies. When that happens, it's up to you to feed the puppies, stimulate them, and keep them warm.

Cow's milk is a poor substitute for bitch's milk, which is more concentrated and has twice the level of protein, almost double the caloric content, and more than twice the content of calcium and phosphorus. Your best bet is to buy a complete puppy formula and enough pet nursing bottles with nipples for your entire litter at a local pet store or veterinary hospital.

Tilt the bottle to prevent the puppy from ingesting air. Don't let it nurse too rapidly. The hole in the nipple should be just large enough to let milk ooze out slowly when the bottle is inverted. Refer to the directions on the product to determine the quantity and frequency you need to feed. To be on the safe side, however, if you need to resort to these measures, you should be following a veterinarian's orders. She can guide you through the correct procedure and teach you how to tube feed the puppies, if necessary.

The puppies will need stimulation to urinate and defecate after each feeding. This is accomplished by gently massaging the anal region with a moistened cotton ball.

Samoyed. *Mary Bloom*

Hand-rearing one or more puppies can be a tremendous task and the chance of losing some of the litter is great. Even though hand-reared puppies are usually very people-oriented, most breeders would leave the early care of puppies to their mothers whenever possible.

Hand-rearing puppies is extremely time-consuming and not without its difficulties. Ready yourself for the probable loss of some members of the litter. A bitch who stubbornly refuses to care for her young probably shouldn't be bred again unless you're ready to assume full responsibility for more puppies in the future.

Weaning the Puppies

The best age to start weaning your litter varies by breed; consult with your breeder or veterinarian for advice. Some puppies begin the weaning process at about three weeks of age. You can start them off by offering a pan of formula in place of their mother's milk. Next, replace the formula with a combination of pablum and formula. Hand-fed puppies may be removed from the bottle at this time, and meat or high-quality canned dog food may be offered in addition to the pablum/formula mixture. At five weeks, discontinue the addition of pablum to the gruel and replace the formula with a solution of equal parts of evaporated milk and water. In addition to the meat and canned food, a good dry or moist commercial dog food can be introduced into the feeding program.

All changes in food or feeding schedules should be made gradually to allow the digestive system time to adjust. A sudden change often leads to diarrhea.

The preceding discussion has barely touched the surface of the basics about breeding and raising a litter to weaning. If you are considering breeding, we advise you to do as much preparation and study as possible. This includes researching the subject and talking with experienced breeders as well as your veterinarian. A good reason to investigate your local dog clubs is to find experienced breeders who can offer good advice and guidance.

Chihuahuas. *Mary Bloom*

Puppies most often learn to eat from a communal food pan. At first, weanlings make an incredible mess of themselves, but by the time they mature, they become very skilled at handling mealtimes.

Boston Terrier. *Mary Bloom*

■ 8 ■

ILLNESS: SIGNS AND SYMPTOMS

Every living thing gets sick at some point in its life, dogs included; it's unfair to expect otherwise. But if you've been careful, and chosen a healthy puppy right from the start, you've built a solid foundation to grow on.

Good preventative care gives your dog as much protection against illness as possible. It grants the dog strength to fight infection, keeps him free from debilitating parasites, and, through regular vaccinations, gives immunity against potentially fatal diseases like distemper and parvovirus. Yearly checkups, which are usually performed when booster shots are given, should not be neglected, since they can detect problems before they become obvious.

But illness can strike any dog at any time. Get to know your dog's normal actions and responses so that something out of the ordinary immediately attracts your attention. And remember that you must act as your dog's interpreter to communicate what's wrong, so be alert and observant at all times.

If your dog exhibits any of the following signs, a visit to the veterinarian is warranted.

- loss of appetite or ravenous appetite without weight gain
- increased thirst and/or frequency of urination
- diarrhea or constipation
- vomiting or gagging
- discharge from the eyes, nose, or mouth
- coughing or respiratory difficulty
- straining to urinate or the production of abnormal urine
- pain, shivering, or fever
- unexplained restlessness or weight loss
- problems with walking or moving

Add to the list anything that is out of the ordinary for *your dog*. You are the best judge of what's normal and what's not.

The next section describes canine illnesses commonly seen by veterinarians. For ease of reference, the following topics are listed alphabetically:

Abscesses; Allergies; Anal irritation; Arthritis; Aural hematoma; Balding; Bladder infection; Bladder stones; Bloat; Bronchitis; Brucellosis; Burns; Cardiomyopathy; Cataracts; Cherry eye; Chronic valvular disease; Color changes; Conjunctivitis; Corneal ulcer; Constipation; Copraphagia (eating stool); Cranial Cruciate Ligament injury; Deafness; Diarrhea; Disc disease; Distemper; Dry eye; Ear infections; Ear mites; Entropion and ectropion; External parasites (fleas, ticks, lice, mites, flies); Flatulence; Foreign bodies; Gastrointestinal problems (general); Gingivitis and dental disease; Glaucoma; Heart problems (including congestive heart failure and congenital heart disease); Heartworm disease; Hip dysplasia; Hot spots; Infections; Kennel cough; Kidney failure (chronic); Lameness; Laryngeal Paralysis; Lip fold infection; Lumps and Bumps; Mammary gland tumors; Mediating luxating patella; Mouth problems; Muscular problems; Neurological problems; Pancreatic exocrine insufficiency; Paralysis; Penis (infection); Pneumonia; Progressive Retinal Atrophy (PRA); Prostatitis; Pyometra; Rabies; Reproductive problems; Respiratory problems; Rhinitis; Ringworm; Seborrhea; Seizures; Skin problems; Soft palate (elongated); Testicle (inflammation); Testicular tumors; Trachea (collapsing); Undescended testicles; Urinary system problems; Vaginal infection; Vomiting; and Watery eyes.

But first, a few more words of warning. *Time* is often the deciding factor in the ability to diagnose and treat an illness. Therefore, we urge you to use this section as a resource in getting to know the canine species—*not* as a guide to diagnosing your own dog. Diseases don't always show up exactly as expected. Let a veterinarian use her professional judgment to diagnose and treat the problem—and the sooner the better.

Abscesses

An abscess is a collection of pus under the skin where an injury has occurred, usually from a bite or puncture wound. The area is often painful, swollen, and red. Abscesses may break open and drain spontaneously, or they may need to be lanced and flushed before proper healing can take place. Never try to squeeze open an abscess. Abscesses should be treated by your veterinarian.

Airedale Terrier. *Mary Bloom*

Allergies

Unlike humans, an allergic dog usually shows the first sign of discomfort through itchy, irritated skin. Some dogs also get a runny nose or eyes, sneeze, or even suffer from vomiting and diarrhea. Uncovering the source of the allergy can be quite frustrating for owners and veterinarians alike.

Some dogs are allergic to components in their diet. A food allergy can emerge early in life; usually the offenders are beef or soy products. The best way to determine whether diet is causing an allergic reaction is to feed hypoallergenic food for several weeks and see if the signs abate. To be altogether certain of a food allergy, you'd need to challenge the dog with the prior food and see if the signs recur.

Another common allergic condition is known as atopy. Atopy refers to an inhalant allergy or a reaction to environmental components. Molds, plants, dust, and even furniture stuffing fall into this category. Signs of atopy may be seasonal. The only practical way to discover what's bothering this allergic dog is to ask a veterinary dermatologist to conduct an intradermal skin test, much as is done with human allergy sufferers. Then you can try avoiding offensive material, or attempt hyposensitization. These problems are also best discussed with a qualified dermatologist.

A few comments about some common dog allergies: Many dogs are sensitive to flea collars, flea bites, or dyes in plastic food dishes. These things are easily identified and corrected. If a flea collar irritates your dog's neck, remove the collar and wash the dog's neck thoroughly with a mild shampoo. Switch to another type of product. We discuss remedies for dealing with fleas, and therefore flea bite allergies, in the section "External Parasites," later in this chapter.

Finally, see if your dog's red, irritated nose is caused by an allergy to dyed plastic by replacing the plastic dish with metal or glass. If it's an allergy, the condition should be resolved.

Anal Irritation

The dog who bites and licks incessantly at the anus or scoots her behind along the floor may be suffering from one of several problems. If soft stools were recently experienced, the anus may be irritated and inflamed secondary to fecal soiling. Some dogs are bothered by insect bites (fleas, for example) or intestinal parasites. A common source of irritation is impaction of the anal sacs.

Finding and eliminating the cause are the first steps to remedying the problem. Meanwhile, provide relief by gently cleaning the anal area using warm, soapy water and applying petroleum jelly or similar soothing salve as needed.

Bloodhound. *Mary Bloom*

Arthritis

The most common form of arthritis in the dog is osteoarthritis, a degenerative disease that causes pain, lameness, and stiffness in the joints. It is frequently seen in older dogs, usually in the large breeds. Grating between joint surfaces may be felt when the limbs are manipulated. X-rays clearly show changes in the bone itself. Aspirin and other medication may provide some relief. A dog suffering from arthritis must have access to soft bedding in a warm, dry environment. Restricted physical activity is essential and the dog must not become overweight.

Aural Hematoma

Aural hematomas are soft swellings that suddenly appear when bleeding has occurred within the cartilage of the ear flap. Rarely painful in themselves, they are usually associated with another problem of the ear such as an infection or injury that caused the dog to violently shake or scratch its head. An autoimmune problem may be at fault. Simply providing drainage will not solve the problem. Most hematomas are surgically opened to remove the blood clot, and then stitched flat until they heal. In fact, left untreated, the blood clot will resolve on its own, but a contracted cauliflower ear will remain.

Balding

Hair loss, when it is not caused by a parasitic condition, trauma, or infection, may result from one of several metabolic disorders. Cushing's syndrome and hypothyroidism are two of the most common.

In Cushing's syndrome, the adrenal glands secrete an excessive amount of cortisol, a hormone. These dogs begin to lose hair on the flank and neck, and may eventually lose hair on the back and sides of the body as well. The skin itself may become thin, scaly, and dry, and may darken in places. Other signs include enlargement of the belly. Typical Cushingoid dogs will want to drink, eat, and urinate more frequently than normal. A complex disorder, Cushing's syndrome is usually treatable.

Hypothyroidism occurs when an inadequate amount of thyroid hormone is released to the body. Dogs with this disease seem to gain weight easily, appear sluggish, and seek out warm spots even during the summer months. Hair changes are more noticeable, and include loss of hair from the flanks and back, increased pigmentation of the skin, scaling, and seborrhea. Because the ears are also commonly affected, you'll often see and smell a thick, greasy, yellowish material inside the canals. Hypothyroidism, once confirmed through a simple blood test, is easily controlled with thyroid hormone supplementation.

Bladder Infection

Bladder infections, or cystitis, frequently occur in both male and female dogs. Individuals suffering from cystitis typically urinate more frequently than normal, usually in small amounts, and blood may be clearly visible in the urine. Urination may appear difficult or painful. Females may also have a vaginal discharge and lick their genital area frequently. A urine sample, sometimes a sterile specimen, is needed to diagnose the problem. Because cystitis is usually caused by a bacterial infection, antibiotics are commonly prescribed for its treatment.

Bladder Stones

Symptoms that suggest the presence of bladder stones are straining or inability to pass urine, recurrent bladder infections, or dribbling urine. Male dogs are most apt to suffer from urinary blockage because their urinary tract is narrow. Some breeds have increased incidence of producing bladder stones. Most stones can be readily identified with an x-ray of the abdomen.

Urinary obstruction is very serious and needs to be relieved as soon as possible via catheterization. Surgery may be required to remove the stones, and medications or dietary restrictions may be prescribed to help prevent further stones from forming.

Bloat

Bloat (acute gastric dilation-torsion) can happen so fast and often proves so deadly that a dog can be gone before you know it. A disease of large, deep-chested dogs, bloat occurs when the stomach fills with gas and/or fluids, then swells and sometimes twists on its own axis. Dogs often go into shock when this happens. Bloat needs to be treated immediately if the dog's life is to be saved.

The history of a dog with bloat often indicates that the dog ate a large meal, drank lots of water, and then exercised within two to three hours after eating. The first sign shown by a dog with impending bloat is often restlessness. The belly appears swollen and firm; tapping gently on it may produce a drumlike sound.

Belgian Malinois. *Mary Bloom*

Immediate surgery is a dog's best chance for survival. The procedure will quickly decompress the stomach and correct any torsion by repositioning the stomach within the abdomen. Intravenous fluids need to be administered to bolster circulation.

Diet and management changes alone will not protect every dog from bloat. However, you can try to help your dog by following these suggestions: (1) Feed small meals, two or three times daily, instead of one large meal, or make dry food available throughout the day and allow the dog to eat at will. (2) Restrict water intake after feeding. (3) Never exercise the dog immediately after it has eaten. If dry food is offered two or three times daily, add water to it first and let the food get soggy so the dog's stomach fills faster and he won't want to drink as much.

Bronchitis

Bronchitis sometimes develops in dogs already suffering from debilitating respiratory infection. Dogs with bronchitis have a dry, rough cough that may persist for days or even weeks. Coughing fits may be so intense that dogs wind up retching afterward. Although they often maintain a normal temperature, dogs with bronchitis have a poor general appearance. Treatment includes antibiotics and rest.

Brucellosis

Canine brucellosis is a bacterial infection spread from one dog to another through close physical contact or ingestion of infected material. Reproductive failure, chiefly abortion, is the main sign of infection. Affected dogs may appear depressed, with a poor coat, enlarged lymph nodes, and swollen joints. Alternatively, there may be no signs of illness at all. Infected male dogs may suffer from inflammation of the scrotum, testicles, or prostate. Dogs who abort or who have difficulty in conceiving should be tested for brucellosis. No effective vaccine has yet been discovered to prevent this disease.

Burns

Oral burns are not unusual, since dogs use their mouths to investigate many new and seemingly tasty objects. Mild oral burns will usually heal themselves. More serious burns, particularly those that occur from ingesting chemical substances, must be brought to the attention of a veterinarian.

Cardiomyopathy

Canine dilated (congested) cardiomyopathy is a disease of large and giant breeds, usually observed in one- to six- year-olds. The heart muscle weakens and degenerates, making blood flow sluggish and resulting in generalized congestive heart failure. The heart itself is greatly enlarged, and is predisposed to irregularities in heart rate. Some heartbeats may actually fail to eject blood into the system. Signs of cardiomyopathy include fatigue, coughing, distention of the abdomen, weight loss, and occasionally swollen legs. Collapse may occur. Drugs can help prolong life, but this is only temporary, since the dramatic changes in the heart are themselves incurable.

Cataracts

Cataracts affect the lens, an internal part of the eye that focuses vision. Relatively common in older dogs, cataracts are readily apparent as distinct opacities (like small marbles) set deep within the eye. Because predisposition to cataract may be an inherited defect, cataracts can actually occur at any age in dogs, and they may also occur secondary to diabetes. The degree of vision loss varies from individual to individual. When blindness is significant, surgical removal of the lens may restore functional vision.

Cherry Eye

All dogs have a tear gland on the inner surface of their third eyelid (the pink membrane that rises from the corner of the eye while your dog is asleep). Occasionally, the gland flips up and protrudes from the corner of the eye. The red, smooth, cherrylike lump doesn't seem to bother most dogs in the least, but can be extremely alarming for owners. Most cases of cherry eye need surgery to either replace or remove the gland.

Chronic Valvular Disease

Valves are tiny pieces of tissue that, by rhythmically snapping open and shut, regulate the flow of blood through the heart. A common form of heart disease, chronic valvular disease occurs when the valves thicken and fail to seal tightly, allowing blood to leak backward. Gradually, the defect compromises the heart's ability to pump, and heart failure develops. Signs of this insufficiency are coughing, difficult or noisy breathing, and restlessness at night. The veterinarian will usually detect a heart murmur.

American Water Spaniel. *Mary Bloom*

Welsh Terrier. *Mary Bloom*

Changes in Skin Color

Some changes in skin color are normal. For instance, some dogs gradually develop spots as they age, usually on areas like the belly, while no other changes are noticed in the skin or body. There are some changes, however, that you should bring to the attention of your veterinarian.

If your dog's skin develops a yellowish cast, for instance, you'll want to have the dog checked out as soon as possible. It may indicate jaundice, which is most often associated with a liver or blood disorder. Jaundice usually accompanies other signs of illness, all of which mean your dog should be examined thoroughly.

Abnormal pallor should also be evaluated by a veterinarian promptly. This usually means anemia, and a veterinarian will attempt to discover the origin of your dog's red blood cell shortage.

Bruising is a normal result of a blunt object injury or, sometimes, having blood drawn. Unexplained or excessive bruising, however, should be discussed with a veterinarian.

Skin will normally undergo hyperpigmentation, or darkening, in response to chronic irritation. If your dog suffers from allergies or any other condition that makes him continually torture the same spot, the skin will eventually thicken and darken to protect itself. The same goes for areas that undergo repeated friction, like the breastbone area of thin-coated dogs or the outer parts of the elbows. These regions will often seem wrinkled, hairless, thick, and blackened—all responses to frequent abuse. Calluses on elbows, hocks, and hip areas may cause problems if they are allowed to persist. The best way to prevent calluses is to provide soft bedding for your dog at all times.

Conjunctivitis

Conjunctivitis is the inflammation of the fleshy membrane that lines the eyelids and covers part of the eyeball. Signs include reddening or swelling of the tissue around the eye and a watery or thick ocular discharge. Conjunctivitis can be bacterial, viral, or allergic in origin, or can result from irritation (a foreign body, for instance, or even a strong gust of wind to the eye). Usually, the problem is readily solved once the cause is identified and appropriate treatment is started.

Corneal Ulcer

The cornea is the clear membrane over the pupil of the eye where, in humans, a contact lens is placed. When something causes a nick or break in the membrane, an ulcer is likely to occur. Ulcers are very painful. Dogs usually hold the affected eye tightly shut, and you will notice an ocular discharge. When examined, the cornea typically looks cloudy in the area of the injury. Corneal ulcers need to be treated without delay to prevent serious complications such as loss of vision.

Constipation

A dog is constipated if she hasn't passed any stool for a day or two. In addition, the dog may strain to defecate without producing any stool. Constipated dogs are often listless, have no appetite, or may begin to vomit if the condition is allowed to persist. Occasionally, a constipated dog may pass watery or bloody material reminiscent of diarrhea despite the fact that the colon is packed with hard stool.

Constipation can occur secondary to eating a diet low in fiber or from ingesting bone chips, grass, paper, or other indigestible matter; having a problem of the prostate gland, having a hernia, or having an inherent problem with the colon. Some dogs seem to be constipation-prone, and must be monitored closely to be sure they pass stool regularly. Other dogs, particularly those with long hair, become mechanically constipated because mats around their anus completely block the passage of feces. Make sure this doesn't happen to your long-haired dog.

Löwchen. *Mary Bloom*

An enema may be needed to soften the stool and allow its expulsion. You may elect to have this done at the veterinary clinic. If you choose to do it at home, a soapy warm water enema is the safest to administer.

A change in diet to include the addition of bran or other fiber-containing substances may help chronically constipated dogs. Commercial dog foods are available to serve this purpose. The veterinarian may also instruct you to add water to your dog's dry food. In addition, you may be advised to withhold bones from your dog.

Copraphagy (Eating Stool)

Coprophagy, or eating stools, is common, especially in young dogs. Nevertheless, this objectionable and unhealthy habit should be discouraged. Adding meat tenderizer to the dog's food works wonders for some dogs, presumably because it imparts a bad flavor to the fecal material. Sometimes changing the diet can solve the problem. If nothing helps, have a veterinarian examine the dog for some form of dietary deficiency. Keeping your dog's area free of feces will obviously help.

Cranial Cruciate Ligament Injury

This common source of sudden rear leg lameness occurs when one of the ligaments inside the knee joint is injured, usually during exercise. Left untreated, the knee remains painful, and arthritis will probably develop in the joint. It is more likely to occur in overweight, adult dogs. Repairing the ligament is a common surgical technique performed at most veterinary practices.

Deafness

Dogs lose their ability to hear from injury, infection, drug reaction, excessive noise, or simply old age. They may also be born deaf or suffer from gradual hearing loss because of a congenital defect. One or both ears may be affected.

Unless complete, deafness is hard to assess in dogs. Obvious signs include difficulty in rousing a dog, or failure of the dog to respond to loud noises made outside his field of vision. With prompt detection, deafness is occasionally curable, as in bacterial infections of the middle or inner ear, or surgical removal of an obstruction in the ear canal. Also, deafness associated with trauma or loud noise may resolve with time.

Diarrhea

Diarrhea is another common symptom in dogs. Mild diarrhea is often treatable at home when it occurs in dogs showing no other signs of illness. Persistent diarrhea, however, means a visit to your veterinarian is warranted. Bring a sample of the stool with you for analysis. If this is impossible, be sure you can give the veterinarian an accurate description of the stool's appearance, amount, and frequency of production. This information can give clues to the origin of the problem.

Many of the reasons dogs come down with uncomplicated diarrhea are comparable to those mentioned in our discussion of vomiting. Unfamiliar food or consuming something indigestible are frequent causes, not to mention stress. More serious reasons include viral gastroenteritis such as coronavirus or parvovirus, for which there are vaccinations. A dog with diarrhea should always be checked for the presence of internal parasites such as worms, coccidia, and giardia.

To treat mild diarrhea at home, withhold food for 24 hours. You may offer small quantities of water. Give the dog Kaopectate or Pepto-Bismol to soothe the intestinal tract. You can start feeding a bland diet the next day. The one described for treating vomiting dogs is fine. If the diarrhea does not respond to this therapy, consult your veterinarian.

Disc Disease

Bad backs trouble some dogs as they do some people, causing pain and incapacitation. Certain breeds are more prone to developing disc disease than others. Observable signs of this disease start when the disc, which normally acts as a cushion between the vertebrae composing the backbone, protrude into the spinal cord area. This very painful condition will cause the dog to acutely reduce her activity, hold her head and neck in a stiff position, and cry out whenever touched. The dog's legs may seem weak or uncoordinated.

Dogs with disc disease must be examined by a veterinarian without delay, in order to decide whether surgery or medical therapy is warranted. Occasionally, disc disease may cause complete paralysis of the hind end.

Distemper

Dogs are routinely vaccinated for immunity against distemper. However, distemper still affects dogs whose owners have not sought to protect their dogs from this virus. Neurological signs of distemper include epileptic-like seizures, snapping of the jaws, and uncontrollable twitching. A thick, yellow discharge from the nose and eyes is observed, and there is a dry cough. Vomiting and diarrhea may also occur. Recovery is possible, but unlikely, once neurological signs are evident.

Dry Eye

Some dogs lack adequate tear production to lubricate and protect the eyes, resulting in keratitis sicca or dry eye. Damage to the cornea may occur. Dry eye is easily diagnosed by measuring tear production on a tiny strip of absorbent paper. It is usually treated with artificial tears, a solution placed in the eye several times daily. Alternatively, a surgical procedure to redirect one of the salivary ducts can help some dogs to lubricate the eyes.

Ear Infections

External ear infections are common, especially in dogs with pendulous ears or ears that contain a lot of hair. The dark, moist environment inherent in these ears encourages bacterial or fungal overgrowth. Parasites, excessive wax, allergies, or foreign material within the ear can also lead to ear problems. Some breeds and individuals are more prone to recurrences of these problems than others.

An infected ear is painful, swollen, and malodorous. The dog may paw at the ear, shake his head, or hold his head tilted toward the ground on the affected side. If you look inside the ear, you may see either dark or puslike material oozing out of the ear canal. The ear will need to be cleaned and medicated, possibly under anesthesia, to remove the discharge as well as any foreign material within the canal. Chronic ear infections are not uncommon. Some cases are best treated surgically to permanently improve exposure to the ear canal for cleaning, circulation of air, and drainage.

Ear Mites

Ear mites are microscopic parasites of the ear canals, where a characteristic coffee ground-like discharge heralds their presence. An intensely itchy condition, ear mite infections are treated with a parasiticidal ear ointment, frequently administered daily for several weeks. Flea powder may also be necessary to kill any mites that have traveled beyond the ear canals.

Entropion and Ectropion

Entropion and ectropion are eyelid abnormalities. In the former, the eyelid (usually the lower lid) rolls toward the eye, permitting the lashes to rub against the cornea and irritate this sensitive structure. Entropion may result from an eyelid injury, but it also occurs as a congenital defect.

The inverse of entropion, ectropion is an eyelid that rolls away from the eyeball. It is usually a problem of dogs with loose facial skin. Ectropion also results from injury or birth defect, or loss of muscle tone in the older dog. Insufficiently protected by this loose eyelid, the eyes of a dog with ectropion are extremely vulnerable to irritation. Corrective surgery is available to repair either of these two eyelid problems.

External Parasites

The following section catalogs the most common external parasites.

Fleas. Fleas are tiny wingless insects that feed on dogs, among other animals. Flea bites make some dogs, who are allergic to the flea saliva, so miserable that they bite and scratch themselves raw. Other dogs do not seem to respond to flea bites with the same intensity. No matter. If you see evidence of fleas on your dog, it is essential to eradicate them as quickly as possible, before their population grows. Hungry fleas sometimes bite humans, too, leaving small, red, itchy bumps most commonly observed on the wrists and ankles.

Spinone Italiano. *The AKC*   **Brussels Griffon.** *Mary Bloom*

How can you tell if your dog has fleas? You may actually see the dark fleas, about the size of sesame seeds, scurrying about on the skin. Their favorite haunts include the base of the ears and the rump. Look closely in sparsely haired places like the groin and stomach for telltale signs. A more accurate way to diagnose fleas, however, when live ones aren't observed, is to part the fur in several places and look for tiny black specks about the size of poppy seeds. These specks are flea feces, composed of digested blood. If you're not sure whether you're looking at "flea dirt" or just plain dirt, place it on a damp piece of white tissue. After a minute or so, a small red spot or halo will become apparent if it is flea feces, since the blood rehydrates and diffuses into the tissue.

The flea comb is a handy item that helps you determine whether your dog has fleas. The teeth are set very close together and snare flea evidence when the comb is drawn through the dog's coat. If you trap a flea, crush it immediately. Though wingless, fleas can jump so fast and so far that they practically disappear the second you see them.

In recent years, humans have managed to get a good handle on the war on fleas. Your veterinarian can advise you as to which products might be suitable for your dog. The days of smelly flea powders are gone, and there are several highly effective methods for keeping your dog flea free. One type of product involves putting a flea prevention product on the dog once every two to three months. Another product requires treating the carpets in the home with a borax-like substance that kills fleas by drying them out.

If you should somehow get an infestation of fleas that needs to be treated, flea bombs set off in each room or living area is an effective way to kill fleas. Premise sprays can also be applied throughout the house. Thorough vacuuming before home treatment is recommended; discard the vacuum cleaner bag once this job is finished. It is important to treat all areas where the dog has traveled, since flea eggs may be present on the floor or furniture. In desperate situations, a yard or kennel spray may be necessary to kill outside fleas.

You must understand that just killing fleas on your dog is not enough to prevent the infestation from repeating itself. The environment must also be treated, as well as any other dogs or cats who live in the household. Also, flea eggs may survive for several weeks after live adults have been eliminated. Repeat treatments may be necessary.

Fortunately, in many parts of the United States, freezing weather goes a long way toward putting an end to outside fleas. In temperate areas, the flea battle may rage year-round. Sometimes it's best to consult a professional exterminator if you should end up with a severe infestation.

Ticks. Ticks are a problem throughout the country, especially in rural and beach areas. This parasite is most widely known for its association with Lyme disease in people and animals. It can also cause anemia, tick paralysis, or other serious blood-borne diseases in the dog. Ticks should be removed as soon as they are discovered, and then destroyed. Make a habit of checking your dog's entire body for ticks, especially the face, ears, feet, and underside. If you are concerned about Lyme disease, bottle any ticks you find and bring them to a veterinarian for identification; not all ticks are known vectors for the disease.

The correct way to remove a tick is to grasp it as close to the skin as possible with a pair of tweezers or hemostats and then pull the tick straight out. Don't touch the tick with your fingers. There's no need to soak the tick first with any chemical products.

Don't be too concerned if you leave a tiny piece of the tick in the skin. It will not grow back and usually does not cause infection. You may notice a small red bump in the area as the skin reacts to the site of attachment. Clean the area daily with hydrogen peroxide and check it for further problems, in which case see the veterinarian.

In light of the seriousness of disease to both human and canine, regular inspection for ticks is well advised, especially in warm weather in areas where ticks are known to be a problem.

Lice. Fortunately, lice infestations are relatively uncommon in the dog. Spread by direct contact with an affected animal, these parasites can cause intense itching. Lice appear as tiny, pale-colored creatures on the surface of the skin. They are easily eradicated with the proper medicated bath, dip, or other product prescribed by a veterinarian.

Mites. Mites are microscopic parasites that inhabit the surface or follicles of the skin. Depending on the type, they can cause mild, moderate, or intense misery. On the other hand, no signs at all may be observed.

One of the most common types of mite infestations of the dog, demodectic mange, causes unsightly skin lesions but ordinarily arouses no response in affected dogs. Usually a problem of young dogs, demodectic mange is suspected when patches of redness and hair loss appear on the forehead, eyes, muzzle, and forepaws. Some dogs outgrow their mange without treatment. Others, however, require the regular use of medicated dips or creams until cured. Demodectic mange can be a serious—and incurable—problem in some dogs, especially older dogs. Dogs with demodectic mange should not be used for breeding, since there appears to be a genetic susceptibility to this problem.

At the other extreme, sarcoptic mange is so itchy that dogs can't seem to control themselves from nonstop scratching. This disease, caused by microscopic scabies or sarcoptic mites, usually causes lesions on the ear, elbows, legs, and face. Left untreated, the whole body may be affected, with thick scaly skin and large areas of hair loss. This serious problem spreads rapidly between dogs and may also affect humans. It must be treated immediately!

Then there are chiggers, tiny beasts found primarily in wooded areas, whose activities cause severe itching and reddening of the skin. Chiggers usually prefer the abdomen, neck, and head (especially the ear flaps and canals). The correct product to eradicate these mites from your dog must be determined by a veterinarian.

The last mite we'll mention is the "walking dandruff," or *Chyletiella yasguri*, mite. Usually a problem of puppies, these mites cause a dandrufflike condition most often seen on the head, neck, and back. There may be mild itching. When they bite humans, these mites leave itchy red spots similar to flea and scabies lesions. The proper medication readily clears up this problem.

Flies. Irritating fly bites cause scabby, crusty sores on the dog's face and ears. Prick-eared dogs are particularly prone to attack by these pests. The sores frequently bleed episodically until they heal, causing owners as well as dogs a lot of grief. When you know flies are apt to be a problem, protect your dog's skin by applying ordinary insect repellent to vulnerable areas. Be sure to avoid contact with the eyes.

The other problem posed by flies is maggots. First, the flies lay their eggs in the dirty, infected skin and ears of a dog. Next, the maggots hatch and begin ingesting the dog's own flesh. It's a terrible situation that can be prevented. If your dog is thick coated, keep a close watch on its body to be sure it is not hiding any wounds. Pay special attention to keeping the anal area clean, free of mats and accumulated stool. Wounds on any dog should be cleaned and treated as soon as possible, especially during the summer, to prevent maggot infestation. If this should occur, maggots must be treated promptly by a veterinarian.

Flatulence

Flatulence can occur after feeding dogs onions, beans, cauliflower, cabbage, soybeans, or other highly fermentable foods. The same applies for diets that include a lot of milk or meat. You may discover that changing the dog's diet will improve the situation. If not, offering a small amount of Digel (simethicone-containing antacid) may provide temporary relief. If all else fails, have your dog checked out for any contributing health problems.

Border Collie. *Chet Jezierski*

Foreign Bodies

A foreign body is something inside the dog's body that doesn't belong there. In the respiratory system, a foreign body can be a stick or burr in the nose or anything that is accidentally inhaled. Foreign bodies in the nasal passages cause incessant pawing at the nose and furious sneezing. There may be a nasal discharge, with or without bleeding. Do not attempt to retrieve foreign bodies from this delicate area yourself. A veterinarian will probably need to sedate or anesthetize the dog in order to do a proper job.

If the foreign body has gone beyond the nasal passage, then the dog will have a sudden, intense coughing fit. This unusual event may clear itself without further problems as the dog coughs it up. If not, however, get to the veterinarian as soon as possible.

When foreign bodies, such as sticks, become lodged in the mouth, especially across the palate, dogs will suddenly paw frantically at their mouths and drool or gag. They may shake their heads and refuse to eat until the object is detected and removed. If you can't locate the trouble, bring the dog to a professional.

The Gastrointestinal System

The gastrointestinal system takes in and processes food, providing energy for sustaining life. The major organs include the stomach and intestines.

Disturbances of the gastrointestinal system probably account for more visits, outside of vaccinations, to veterinarians. It's virtually certain that someday, during the course of your dog's lifetime, she will suffer a bout of vomiting or diarrhea. Other signs of gastrointestinal upset include regurgitation, constipation, unusual stools, or flatulence. Because a dog with a gastrointestinal disturbance usually feels uncomfortable, she may act restless or drool excessively, or need to drink or urinate more frequently than normal.

Gingivitis and Dental Disease

Poor oral hygiene causes gum and tooth disease in many dogs. Dogs in need of help have blatant signs: the teeth look terrible, the gums are swollen and may bleed easily, the breath smells foul, and you may see excessive drooling. When the roots of the rear teeth are affected, facial swelling commonly occurs.

Regular oral inspection and dental cleaning is important. Despite your best efforts, however, professional cleaning will probably be needed from time to time. Also, some oral diseases are linked to more serious problems like diabetes or kidney disease.

Glaucoma

Glaucoma is caused by increased pressure within the eyeball. As the pressure climbs, tissues within the eyes are destroyed, leading to partial or complete blindness. Dogs with glaucoma may squint or stare; the eyes seem to be enlarged, with reddening of the white part of the eye (the sclera) and a hazy appearance to the inside of the eye. This serious condition is quite painful, and requires immediate veterinary attention.

Heart Problems—General

The rhythmic pumping of the muscular heart circulates blood through the body. Blood provides the body with vital nutrients like oxygen, electrolytes, and hormones, which regulate body functions. It also carries away the waste products of metabolism, including carbon dioxide. Heart disease may be either acquired (developed after birth) or congenital (present at birth). Specialized equipment like the EKG and echocardiograph, as well as x-rays and auscultation, may be necessary to determine the exact nature of each form of heart disease.

Each time you visit the veterinarian, he should check your dog's heart for abnormal sounds and for irregularities in rhythm or frequency of beats. The pulse should also be evaluated for strength and synchronicity with each contraction of the heart.

Cocker Spaniel. *Mary Bloom*

Signs that may indicate a heart problem are coughing and shortness of breath, lethargy, weakness, distended abdomen, and/or swollen limbs. If your dog suffers from fainting spells, stunted growth, or weight loss, or if you notice a bluish color of its gums, be sure to seek veterinary advice.

Heart Problems—Congenital Heart Diseases

Congenital heart diseases are functional cardiac problems that are present at birth. Your first indication of a defect may occur at the time of the puppy's initial veterinary examination, when abnormal heart sounds are detected. Heart failure may also present itself at an early stage. Here are just a few examples of congenital defects.

One form of congenital heart defect is *patent ductus arteriosus.* This refers to the presence of a vessel—which should ordinarily close shortly after birth—connecting the pulmonary artery to the aorta. The vessel gives blood a way to bypass the lungs, so there's less oxygenated blood going to the body. A distinct heart murmur is noticed upon ausculting the chest. The only effective treatment is surgical repair.

Defects also occur in newborn pups. These are small openings in the muscular wall separating the two major pumping chambers of the heart. The hole can vary in size. Surgical correction is possible at specialized veterinary institutions.

A constrictive abnormality that obstructs the passage of blood out of the right ventricle into the pulmonary artery is known as *pulmonic stenosis.* This defect increases the workload of the heart and may cause heart failure. Some types of stenosis can be partially relieved by surgery.

Heart Problems—Congestive Heart Failure

Heart failure occurs when the heart can't deliver a sufficient quantity of oxygenated blood to meet the body's demands. The term "congestive" refers to an abnormal amount of fluid accumulating outside of the vessels, as in the lungs. When this happens, for example, the dog may begin to cough and show shortness of breath. He may be unable to tolerate excitement or exercise, and the abdomen may start to enlarge as fluid accumulates in this body compartment as well. Congestive heart failure, once diagnosed, may be treated with drugs to strengthen contractions of the heart, expand the vascular capacity, and promote excretion of retained fluids through diuresis. Feeding a special low-salt diet is usually recommended to help lessen problems of fluid retention.

English Fox Hound. *Mary Bloom*

Heartworm Disease

This disease is caused by actual worms inhabiting the chambers of the heart. Heartworms gain entry to the dog's circulatory system through the bite of a carrier mosquito. Eventually, adult worms migrate to the heart and arteries leading to the lungs. Since worms may grow to 12 inches long, it is not surprising that they both physically obstruct blood flow and damage the pulmonary arteries, making it difficult for the heart to pump blood through the lungs. Heart failure and severe lung damage can occur in heavily infested dogs. Heartworm disease can be treated with arsenic-containing drugs to eradicate the adult worms, followed by other drugs to kill immature worms, and long periods of forced rest. It's better to prevent heartworm infestation in the first place by giving preventative medications during the warm months of the year.

Miniature Schnauzer. *Mary Bloom*

Hip Dysplasia

We could easily devote pages to hip dysplasia, because it is common and is so great a source of heartbreak, especially to owners of larger dogs. Hip dysplasia is a congenital defect with potential environmental and nutritional influences. Basically, hip dysplasia is malformation of the hip joint. Dogs with this condition show hip pain, limping, or a swaying gait. Some animals develop signs during the rapid growth that occurs from four to nine months of age, while others fall victim later in life. Other indications of hip dysplasia include hearing a clicking noise while the dog walks or noticing the dog wince when its hindquarters are touched. Affected dogs are typically slow to rise from a seated position.

The diagnosis is made through orthopedic examination and x-rays of the hip joints. Affected dogs should be maintained at proper weight, to reduce the carrying load on the hindquarters. Their bedding should be kept in a warm, dry place, and their exercise should be restricted. The development of arthritis is a serious concern for dogs with hip dysplasia. Medication can help alleviate the pain of this disease, but surgery (or euthanasia) is sometimes the only humane choice. Lastly, hip dysplasia is an inherited disease, so dogs with confirmed hip dysplasia should *never* be used for breeding.

Hot Spots

One of the most common summertime complaints seen by veterinarians are hot spots, round hairless patches of tender, red, oozing skin that seem to erupt overnight. They are usually found on the rump, although they may appear anywhere on the body. Hot spots are especially prevalent in heavy-coated breeds and in any dog with skin allergies.

Hot spots probably begin as a focus of irritation caused by a flea bite, impacted anal sacs, or other small annoyances. However, the more the dog licks and chews at the spot, the worse it feels, so the more the animal licks and chews. A small problem explodes into a large one. These lesions need to be treated promptly before you have a dog in agony.

Treatment of a hot spot begins with clipping away the surrounding hair and cleaning the surface of the wound. The area is then covered with a soothing spray, liquid, or ointment. The veterinarian will attempt to find and eliminate the source of the complaint. Your dog may need to wear an Elizabethan collar around his neck, to prevent him from attacking the area further, until the skin begins to heal. Antibiotics and anti-inflammatory medications may be prescribed as well.

Infections

Skin infections usually result from damage to the skin by a cut, puncture, or scrape. If it is a primary infection, however, the most common presentations are single or multiple areas of red patches resembling a rash or small bumps similar to pimples. There may or may not be itching. Skin infections of this type are usually caused by staphylococcus bacteria and may need to be treated with antibiotics or medicated baths.

Ignoring a skin injury may turn a small problem into a large one through bacterial infection. Infected wounds are painful, red, and swollen. They feel warm to the touch and may have an abnormal, pus-like discharge. A foul odor may originate from the infected wound. Seek appropriate treatment, such as local wound care and antibiotics, for this condition.

Kennel Cough

Otherwise known as *infectious canine tracheobronchitis,* kennel cough is a common respiratory problem in dogs. It readily spreads from one individual to another. Many dogs come down with kennel cough after boarding or some other situation where they have been in close proximity to other dogs. Carriers are often asymptomatic.

Signs include a dry, hacking cough sometimes accompanied by a mild nasal discharge. Most dogs remain bright and alert despite their alarming coughing spells, and will spontaneously recover within a few weeks. However, to be on the safe side, most veterinarians prescribe a short course of antibiotics to protect their patients from further harm. Consider asking for a kennel cough vaccination if your dog is going to be staying in a kennel.

Kidney Failure (Chronic)

Kidney failure can happen at any stage of a dog's life, but it is much more common in older dogs. Typical signs include excessive drinking and urination, weight and appetite loss, and vomiting. As waste products accumulate in the blood, the dog becomes listless, weak, and depressed. Without therapy, dogs with kidney failure will die. One of the primary therapeutic measures for kidney failure is intravenous fluid therapy, which requires hospitalization. Kidney disease, whether congenital or acquired, usually carries a grave prognosis for a normal life expectancy.

Lameness

There are many reasons why dogs limp. Fractures, dislocations, ligamentous injuries, congenital defects, and just plain soreness are merely a few. Most of the time, minor limping disappears if the dog has a couple of days of restricted activity and perhaps aspirin for pain relief. If you suspect that trauma has played a role in causing the lameness, or your dog seems to be in serious discomfort, a quick visit to the veterinarian is in order. X-rays may be necessary to verify the existence of a problem. Sometimes tranquilization is required to obtain a good x-ray image of the area, so try to withhold food from the dog before you go to the veterinarian.

Laryngeal Paralysis

Laryngeal paralysis is a problem of large dogs in their middle to old age. The first sign may be occasional noisy breathing, especially when the dog has been excited or exercised. Respiratory difficulty may progress to complete inability to breathe. Sometimes surgery is required to alleviate this problem involving the tissue in the back of the throat.

Lip Fold Infection

This problem affects dogs with loose skin around the mouth, where small pools of food and saliva accumulate. It also happens when mouth injuries become infected, or when licking spreads an infection from another part of the body to the mouth. If your dog begins to drool a thick, odorous substance or paws at her mouth, check the skin around the lips. Always try to keep the lip folds as clean as possible, especially following a meal, to prevent the onset of an infection.

Lumps and Bumps

Finding a single lump or bump on your dog's skin is not necessarily reason to panic. Most skin masses are not malignant, and once removed, they do not recur. Some are inconsequential and may be left alone. A wart is a good example of this type of bump; ordinarily they may be ignored, unless owners find them unsightly or they cause the dog discomfort because of their location.

However, every abnormal mass discovered in your dog's skin should be a matter for concern. Let a veterinarian decide whether or not to pursue a diagnostic workup. Because malignancies are a consideration, especially in older dogs, don't waste time before seeking veterinary advice.

Tibetan Terrier. *Mary Bloom*

Viszla. *Mary Bloom*

Mammary Gland Tumors

Tumors of the mammary gland, or breast, are among the most common neoplasms found in female dogs. Approximately half of the tumors are malignant. Remember that this type of cancer is almost entirely preventable by spaying a bitch when she is young.

Mammary gland tumors usually appear as small, firm nodules located most often in the nipples nearest to the hind legs. They can occur singly or in groups, and may exhibit rapid growth. Owners of unspayed bitches should examine their dog's abdomen regularly and bring any lumps to the attention of a veterinarian. Surgery is usually performed to remove the tumors. A biopsy will determine whether the tissue is malignant or benign. Veterinarians usually x-ray the dog's chest prior to surgery to check for evidence of related cancer in the lungs.

Medial Luxating Patella

The patella, or kneecap, is a small saucer of bone that glides up and down in front of the knee joint. Because of functional abnormalities, the patella of some small dogs slides toward the inner leg. Off track, the errant patella causes sudden (and often painless) episodes of limping.

Dogs with this condition may need surgical correction of one or both knees to relieve the problem once and for all. Otherwise, the knee may become arthritic. Obesity as well as excessive exercise should always be avoided, since both will aggravate the problem.

Mouth Problems

The mouth aids in respiration and initiates the chain of events that brings nourishment to the rest of the body. A problem with the mouth is suspected when dogs exhibit unusual drooling or oral discharge, head shaking, bleeding, or pawing at the mouth. Bad breath, inflammation, growths, or difficulty in swallowing may also point toward oral disease.

Muscular Problems

The musculoskeletal system supports, protects, and moves the dog's body. In addition, the bones provide a site for mineral and fat storage, and house the marrow, which produces red blood cells. When something goes wrong with the muscles, tendons, ligaments, or bones, the signs are usually obvious. Limping, weakness, pain, or stiffness indicate a problem in the musculoskeletal system, as do swollen joints or any change in the way your dog moves.

Neurological Problems

The neurological system is composed of the brain, spinal cord, and nerves. It receives, conducts, and interprets sensory information and distributes messages that control the activity of muscles and other organs. Uncoordination, weakness, changes in muscle tone, and paralysis are signs of a neurological problem. Other indications include seizures, sensory abnormalities, and sudden bizarre behavior changes.

Pancreatic Exocrine Insufficiency

The typical dog with pancreatic exocrine insufficiency (PEI) has an enormous appetite but never seems to gain weight. Its stools are usually voluminous, soft, light colored, and may appear greasy or oily due to high amounts of undigested fats and proteins. Dogs with PEI are unable to produce certain enzymes in the pancreas, enzymes that would promote normal digestion and absorption of nutrients. PEI is treated with lifelong supplementation of pancreatic enzymes, usually added directly to the food, along with the feeding of a low-fat, moderate-protein diet.

Paralysis

Partial or complete paralysis may be caused by several diseases in dogs. One of the most common, outside of traumatic injury, is intervertebral disc disease. The problem arises when discs apply pressure on the spinal cord (see Muscular Problems). Neurological messages between the brain and body parts are affected, and paralysis may follow.

Other degenerative diseases that involve changes in the spine, most often observed in large breeds, can cause paralysis, as can growing tumors and disorders of the peripheral nerves. A veterinarian will need to perform a special neurological examination, in conjunction with other diagnostic tests, to determine the origin of the paralysis.

Penis (Infection)

Most mature male dogs normally discharge a small amount of white or yellowish material from the skin covering the penis, known as the prepuce. However, if a dog licks frequently at the prepuce, or produces an excessive, discolored, or odorous discharge, then an infection of the penis (balanoposthitis) is likely. The penis may appear intensely red and be covered with small bumps. Antibiotics and douches are commonly used to eliminate the infection.

Curly-Coated Retriever. *Mary Bloom*

Pneumonia

A very serious disease that can be caused by a virus, bacteria, allergy, or parasite, pneumonia needs to be treated without delay. Signs include coughing, rapid breathing, a high fever, and a quick pulse. You may or may not actually hear a rattling or bubbling noise within the dog's chest.

Progressive Retinal Atrophy

Progressive retinal atrophy (PRA) is a genetic disease in which the cells of the retina gradually degenerate, leading to loss of sight. Many breeds are affected by this devastating disease. Predicting the onset of blindness is breed-dependent, but it may occur at from several months to several years of age.

The first indication of PRA is loss of night vision. With dogs, owners first notice behavioral changes linked to situations in which light is limited. The disease then progresses over a period of months to years, but the outcome is blindness. Unfortunately, there is no known treatment for PRA.

Prostatitis

Non-neutered male dogs may encounter prostatic enlargement or infection (prostatitis), showing signs of difficult or painful urination. Dogs with prostatitis are ordinarily feverish, drip blood or pus from the preputial opening, and may stand in a pained, hunched-up posture. A bacterial infection, prostatitus is treated with appropriate antibiotics. It can become chronic in some male dogs.

Pyometra

Another disease of the unspayed bitch, pyometra is a serious uterine infection in which the uterus fills up with pus. It is usually seen in females over six years old, but can occasionally occur in younger animals. Pus may be clearly visible emerging from the bitch's genitals.

Bitches affected with pyometra are commonly depressed, and may vomit. Related signs are increased thirst and frequency of urination. Pyometra can be fatal if it is not treated promptly. Usually, emergency surgery to remove the infected uterus is required. Other methods of treatment are occasionally tried for valuable bitches intended for breeding.

Rabies

Rabies is caused by a virus transmitted by contact with infected saliva, usually from the bite of a rabid animal (skunks, foxes, bats, and raccoons are typical carriers). There is little chance of survival once the virus starts reproducing within the body. Dogs are a primary source of rabies in humans; you must maintain up-to-date rabies vaccinations in your dog.

The first sign of rabies in an infected animal is usually a marked personality change. In contrast to his ordinary behavior, the dog may seem overly affectionate or shy; he may appear restless or become aggressive. Many dogs become sensitive to light, their eyes dilated. In addition, they often run a fever, have diarrhea, or vomit.

Dogs with the paralytic form of rabies lose their muscle control, so the jaw may hang down and the tongue may protrude. The dog may drool, cough, paw at the mouth, or demonstrate a voice change. Eventually the rabid dog loses coordination, collapses, enters a coma, and dies. There is no treatment for rabies in the dog.

Reproductive Problems

The reproductive system includes the sexual organs, both internal and external, of male and female dogs. Infertility is only one indication of a problem with this system. Other symptoms include abnormal discharge from the penis or vulva, and swelling, inflammation, or pain involving the reproductive organs.

Respiratory Problems

The respiratory system includes those organs involved in the process of breathing. These are parts you can see, like the nose and mouth, as well as internal organs such as the trachea, bronchi, and lungs.

Problems with respiration may originate anywhere along this pathway. Symptoms of respiratory distress include nasal discharge, coughing, or sneezing. Noisy or difficult breathing also indicates an abnormality, as do any changes in voice quality or irregular sounds that seem to come from the throat or chest.

Rhinitis

Rhinitis is another word for infection of the nasal passages. Dogs with this problem have a thick, foul-smelling nasal discharge from one or both nostrils. Treatment depends on the origin of the problem;

infected maxillary teeth are a common culprit, although it may be more serious than that. Antibiotics are typically used to help clear up the infection.

Ringworm

Despite its name, ringworm is not a squirming parasite but rather a fungal infection of the skin. Ringworm lesions appear as circular, hairless patches of scaly skin. Stubby bits of broken grayish hair may be found within and along the edges of these areas. Severely affected dogs may have diseased areas incorporating large portions of the body. To diagnose ringworm, a culture may be taken from a sample of crust and hair. Proper diagnosis and treatment is especially important since ringworm can spread to people.

Seborrhea

Seborrheic skin is flaky and scaly, and may feel either excessively dry or oily. Secondary infections are not uncommon, especially in the case of oily seborrhea, in which case you may notice a rancid smell emanating from the skin. Seborrhea may be complicated by other problems like hypothyroidism. True seborrhea is an incurable but controllable problem; for example, regular bathing in special shampoos can help eliminate the scaling and oiliness of the skin.

Sealyham Terriers. *Mary Bloom*

Seizures

Seizures are frequently caused by epilepsy, although they may be due to viral, bacterial, or fungal infections, as well as brain tumors or head trauma. During seizures, dogs typically appear to lose consciousness, fall on their sides, vocalize, paddle their legs, and frequently urinate and/or defecate (although any bizarre behavior can be part of a seizure).

Epilepsy occurs when a focus in the brain suddenly fires for no apparent reason, setting off a flurry of messages in the sensitive brain tissue. Although seizures are distressing to observe, especially for the first time, most are rarely life-threatening. A dog exhibiting seizures should be examined thoroughly by a veterinarian to try to determine their cause. If the diagnosis is epilepsy, oral medication (usually phenobarbital) can help minimize the recurrence of seizures.

Skin Problems

The skin is the largest organ of the dog's body and a frequent source of problems. The job of the skin is to protect the inner organs and tissues from invasions by foreign substances, changing temperature, and dehydration. The skin also works to synthesize essential vitamins for the rest of the body and performs the indispensable job of processing information about the external world through sensation.

Normal canine skin is smooth and flexible. Colors range from pale pink to brown to bluish black. Spotted skin is normal in any dog, even those coats that are uniform in color. Lumps, bumps, scabs, patches of hair loss, or parasites shouldn't be visible anywhere on a healthy dog's body.

Dogs have seasonal shedding cycles, which don't always behave according to a strict schedule. There are so many different kinds of canine hair that it's difficult to draw a typical picture. Obviously the hair of a Miniature Schnauzer shouldn't grow in like that of a Golden Retriever! Perhaps it's best to concentrate on what hair shouldn't be. It shouldn't break or pull out easily, or seem excessively dry or oily. In a smooth-coated dog, the coat should not appear dull or weak. Any sudden or significant change in the hair's appearance should be brought to the attention of your veterinarian.

Soft Palate (Elongated)

An elongated soft palate is most often seen in short-faced breeds. It causes nasal discharge and noisy breathing because the air passages are obstructed. These dogs typically breathe through the mouth, produce

The English Setter is an elegant, active, and rugged gun dog. By nature, he is gentle, affectionate, and friendly. *The American Kennel Club*

The Siberian Husky was developed in Asia as a sled dog. He is friendly and gentle, but also alert and outgoing. *Mary Bloom*

The Basset Hound, an old, aristocratic breed, emerged from relative obscurity to become one of the most publicized and characterized breeds. He is renowned for his sweet personality and gentle manners. *Mary Bloom*

The Shiba Inu was originally developed for hunting by sight and scent in the mountainous regions of Japan. Alert and agile with keen senses, he is an excellent watchdog and companion. *Mary Bloom*

The Poodle originated in Germany as a water retriever. He comes in three sizes: Toy, Miniature, and Standard. Active, intelligent, and elegant in appearance, the poodle is a popular pet and companion around the world.
Mary Bloom

The Chesapeake Bay Retriever is one of a small number of breeds that originated here in America. Valued as both a companion and a gun dog, he is known for his happy disposition, intelligence, quiet good sense, and affectionate, protective nature.
Beth Hanson

The Italian Greyhound is the smallest of the family of Sight Hounds. Prized for his beauty, small size, and affectionate disposition, he readily adapts to most households. *Kent and Donna Dannen*

The Chow Chow was bred in China as an all-purpose dog used for hunting, herding, pulling, and protection of the home. Primarily a companion today, he is highly intelligent and extremely loyal to his owner. *Mary Bloom*

The Shih Tzu is an elegant, aristocratic dog from China. He was cherished by the royals there for more than 1,000 years, and is believed to have descended from the Lhasa Apso and the Pekingese. *Kent and Donna Dannen*

The Flat-Coated Retriever is a self-reliant hunter who has the Newfoundland, the setter, the sheepdog, and spaniel-like water dogs in his ancestry. As a family member, he is sensible, alert, and highly intelligent. *Kent and Donna Dannen*

The Weimaraner originated as a hunting dog bred strictly by and for aristocrats. Originally used to hunt game such as wolves, mountain lions, and bears, today birds are his main prey. *Tara Darling*

The Tibetan Spaniel is one of the breeds whose original function was to guard the monasteries of Tibet. Today, sitting on a high spot and watching what everyone is doing is still a favorite activity of the breed. *Mary Bloom*

The Lhasa Apso originated in the mountains of Tibet, working as guards of the Buddhist monasteries. Best known for his long, lustrous coat, he is happy and assertive, but wary of strangers. *The American Kennel Club, photo by Audrey Pavia*

The Greyhound, depicted in the times of ancient Egypt, can be traced in the varying terrains of almost every country and continent on the globe. Among the earliest of exhibits at American dog shows, 18 were entered in the first Westminster Kennel Club in 1877. *The American Kennel Club, photo by Audrey Pavia*

The Puli has played an important part in the lives of Hungarian shepherds for more than 1,000 years. By nature, he is an affectionate, intelligent, and home-loving companion. *Mary Bloom*

The Great Dane is known as the Apollo of dogs. His regal appearance combines dignity, strength, and elegance with great size and power. This giant breed is spirited, courageous, friendly, and dependable. *Kent and Donna Dannen*

The English Cocker Spaniel, one of the oldest types of land spaniels known, is an active and merry sporting dog. Neither sluggish nor hyperactive, he is a willing worker and a faithful and engaging pet and companion. *Tara Darling*

The Smooth Fox Terrier, like the Wire, was originally bred to participate in the sport of fox hunting. He presents a merry, lively, and active appearance. *Beth Hanson* snorting noises, and snore while sleeping. Signs are exacerbated by hot weather, physical exertion, or other stressful conditions. In most cases, surgery corrects the problem by shortening the soft palate.

Testicle (Inflammation)

Orchitis, or inflammation of the testicle, may result from an external injury or internal disease. The outcome of this painful condition may be infertility. Inflamed testicles appear firm and enlarged. They are extremely sensitive. The dog shows difficulty in walking and may prefer to sit on cold surfaces. Orchitis must be treated promptly to preserve fertility in a breeding dog.

Testicular Tumors

There are three general types of testicular tumors, with varying potential for malignancy. If you notice any change in the appearance or consistency of your dog's testicles, have the dog examined by a veterinarian. The treatment for testicular tumors is castration.

Trachea (Collapsing)

Usually a disease of small dogs, symptoms of a collapsed trachea include noisy breathing and frequent coughing. Sometimes dogs seem incapable of catching their breath.

Manchester Terrier. *Mary Bloom*

The trachea is normally a rigid tube. In an affected dog, however, the trachea is somewhat soft, so it tends to narrow from time to time. This obviously impedes air flow. Most dogs learn to live with their problem, as do their owners, once they understand that it is rarely life-threatening. Obesity, stress, and pressure on the trachea should be avoided. Surgery can help severely affected animals.

Undescended Testicles

Both testicles should be in the scrotum by the time a puppy is six months old. Failure of one or both testicles to descend is abnormal, and the affected individual has a higher risk of developing testicular tumors later in life. These dogs should be neutered (the surgeon will locate and remove the "missing" testicle)—both for the dog's health and for the prevention of breeding, since this defect can be inherited.

Urinary System Problems

The urinary system includes the kidneys and ureters, bladder, prostate (in male dogs) and urethra. The kidneys are the major organs, maintaining correct water and mineral balance, and excreting waste products of metabolism.

Maltese. *Mary Bloom*

Polish Lowland Sheepdog. *Mary Bloom*

Excessive drinking and urination are often the first signs observed by owners of dogs with urological problems. Other signs include straining or inability to urinate, frequent urination of small amounts, blood in the urine, and uncontrollable urination. Dogs with kidney pain will sometimes stand in a hunched-up posture. Weight loss, loss of appetite, and vomiting are also potential indications of kidney disease.

Vaginal Infection

Female dogs who lick excessively at their genitals and produce an abnormal vaginal discharge that stains the hair around the vulva may have vaginitis. These bitches may also seem unusually attractive to male dogs. In young females, the infection may be characterized by only small amounts of discharge and signs of painful urination. Antibiotics and douches are used to treat the problem.

Vomiting

Dogs vomit for myriad reasons; some are more serious than others. If your dog vomits once or twice but seems healthy in every other respect, there is probably no need to worry. Occasional uncomplicated vomiting is caused by change of diet, garbage ingestion, or eating plant material. If you restrict food for a day and give your dog a little Pepto-Bismol, the problem will probably disappear on its own. Feed a bland diet such as baby food or boiled chopped meat combined with plain white rice (pour the fat off before you mix the two together) for a few days more.

Canaan Dog. *Mary Bloom*

If, however, your dog has frequent forceful vomiting, or vomits in conjunction with other signs such as diarrhea, depression, or collapse, get the animal to the veterinarian. This also goes for vomiting in which blood or other unusual substances are observed. Potential causes for these types of vomiting may include viral infections, foreign body obstructions, tumors, pancreatitis, renal or liver disease, and so forth.

Watery Eyes

Excessive tearing is seen most often in the small breeds. The resulting moisture around the eyes and down the sides of the face contributes to local inflammation or infection of the underlying skin. The discharge often stains surrounding hair an ugly brown color; this is especially obvious in white or light-colored dogs.

Watery eyes can result from a variety of causes, the most common being irritation to the eye and inadequate tear drainage. Removing the source of the irritation, such as excessive hair around the eyes, treating infection with antibiotics, or flushing the masolacrimal drainage system can help eliminate the problem.

Plott Hound. *Mary Bloom*

▪ 9 ▪

FIRST AID

First aid is the immediate action taken in an emergency before you can reach a veterinarian. It can help prevent injuries from worsening, alleviate pain, or even save your dog's life. First aid, however, is a *preliminary* measure—it should never replace professional care. If you should find yourself in any of the following emergency situations, you should stabilize your dog and then get to a veterinarian as soon as possible.

The following pages describe what to do in some common emergencies. First aid situations usually call for fast action. The number one rule is don't panic.

Be prepared. Familiarize yourself with first aid techniques before an actual crisis happens. The telephone number of your veterinarian or veterinary emergency hospital should always be posted near the phone, along with your other emergency numbers. Notify the veterinarian that you are on your way with an animal and describe the nature of the problem so preparation can be made for your arrival. Actions such as these can greatly improve your pet's chances for survival.

If your dog has a medical emergency or has been in an accident, remember that in order to care for the dog, you must keep yourself safe. If your dog is in trouble, needs your help, and is trying to bite out of fear, you will need to muzzle the dog. Once you've decided that the dog will not bite you or you've applied a muzzle, you need to make sure the dog is in a safe place. If the dog has been hit by a car, getting the dog out of the road is an obvious priority. A few tips for applying a homemade emergency muzzle and for moving an injured dog follow.

American Staffordshire Terrier. *Mary Bloom*

Making a Muzzle

Even a loving and trusted dog may bite when hurt and frightened. The best way to ensure your safety while trying to help or restrain an injured dog is to apply a muzzle.

Constructing an emergency muzzle with panty hose, a gauze bandage, a necktie, or piece of rope about two feet long is not difficult. Begin by tying a loose knot in the middle of the material, leaving a large loop. Then slip the loop over the dog's snout and tighten the knot over the bridge of the nose. Bring the ends down under the chin, tie a knot there, and then bring the ends around back of the ears. Finish by securely tying a bow behind the ears. The muzzle will not interfere with breathing if tied in this manner, and can be released quickly by loosening the bow and pulling the material straight from the nose.

Moving an Injured Dog

An injured dog must be carried so that further damage is avoided. Dogs of any size may be placed on a towel or blanket, which is then lifted by its edges. Or they may be gently laid on a firm surface of sufficient size, such as a plywood board, before being transported. Smaller dogs can be wrapped gently in warm material and carried in one's arms or in a sturdy box.

Always exercise caution when attempting to pick up and support an injured animal. If you haven't muzzled the dog, he may try to bite you, or you may inadvertently worsen matters by carrying him improperly. As always, use common sense.

Common Medical Emergencies

The most common medical emergencies listed in alphabetical order are: bite wounds (from dog bites); bleeding; breathing problems (the dog has stopped breathing); broken bones (fractures); heart trouble (no heartbeat); heatstroke; poisoning; seizures; shock; and topical irritants. Let's have a look at each problem and some things you should do if this happens to your dog.

Bite Wounds

Dogfights commonly occur when owners are not paying proper attention. Don't let your dog roam. He should be on a leash at all times when outdoors and off your property. If a fight should occur, try to separate the dogs as best you can without placing yourself at risk; sometimes dousing dogs with water startles them enough to stop a fight. Remove other dogs from the vicinity to reduce the frenzy.

The wounds sustained in a dogfight may look minor, but the puncture wounds caused by dog teeth can quickly develop into major infections. Small puncture wounds are a misleading indication of the damage to muscle and other underlying tissues. Bite wounds must be thoroughly cleaned and flushed with an agent like hydrogen peroxide; often debridement and/or drains are necessary to effect a cure. Treatment may be extensive. Seek veterinary help immediately.

Longhaired Dachshund. *Mary Bloom*

Bleeding

External bleeding may be controlled by applying a pressure dressing, which you can make out of strips of gauze or other sturdy fabric. Wrap the injured area with the bandage material, applying even pressure as you work. Watch for tissue swelling below the wound—a sign of blocked circulation. Should this happen, you must loosen or remove the bandage. Avoid using elasticized bandage material, if possible.

If no bandage material is available, place pressure directly on the wound with your hand or a clean piece of cloth to help block the flow of blood.

When serious bleeding occurs, such as when an artery has been severed, you may need to apply a tourniquet in addition to a pressure bandage. Tourniquets may be fashioned from loops of rope, gauze, or cloth—anything that can be wrapped tightly around the area above the wound to interrupt the blood supply. If you are forced to use a tourniquet, you must loosen the pressure every 10 minutes or so, or else the tissues will suffer from lack of oxygen.

Breathing Problems—Artificial Respiration

When a dog has stopped breathing, artificial respiration may be necessary. Be extremely careful, since your face will be very close to the dog's mouth (and teeth). Even dogs in respiratory arrest can reflexively close their jaws without warning.

Chinese Shar-Pei. *Mary Bloom*

Open the dog's mouth and check for obstructions. Extend the dog's tongue and look into the throat and make sure that, too, is clear. Remove any fluid from the mouth that might interfere with the passage of air. Then close the mouth and continue to hold it gently closed.

Now inhale. Completely cover the dog's nose with your mouth and exhale gently; don't blow hard! Carefully blow air into the lungs and watch the chest for expansion. Repeat every five to six seconds, or 10 to 12 breaths per minute.

Broken Bones—Fractures

Fractured bones are very painful but not always immediately obvious. If you suspect your dog has a fracture, carefully transport him to the veterinarian on a rigid board or use other means of support, avoiding stress on the injured area. If a limb is fractured, position it on a cushion, wrap it in a rolled-up magazine, or just gently support it in your hand (muzzle the dog as a precaution) to avoid more serious injury.

Compound fractures, characterized by the bone piercing the skin, are more serious and more susceptible to infection. Immediately cover the area with a clean piece of material and then get emergency help.

Heart Trouble—Heart Massage

Heart massage is attempted when you can't detect a heartbeat. It should be combined with artificial respiration. A basic course in CPR will help you learn how to perform this potentially lifesaving technique on both animals and people.

To begin, lay the dog on his right side, and place two hands over the heart area. Press firmly on the chest about 70 times per minute. In the case of a small dog, place one hand on either side of the chest near the elbow instead. Stay calm, and avoid breaking the dog's ribs by pressing too hard as you try to reestablish a heartbeat.

Heatstroke

Heatstroke affects dogs whose body temperatures climb way above normal range. Tragically, most cases of heatstroke occur when owners close their dogs in cars with the windows rolled up, or confine them to other poorly ventilated areas on hot, humid days. It only takes a few minutes for heatstroke to develop.

A dog with heatstroke breathes rapidly but takes shallow breaths. The heartbeat is also very rapid. If not already collapsed, the dog looks close to it. The body temperature is typically well above 104 degrees.

It is crucial to cool an animal suffering from heatstroke as soon as possible and treat shock and other complications, which accompany this condition.

The most effective way to begin lowering the dog's temperature is to spray him with cool water and place ice against the groin, belly, head and neck. Wrap cold, wet towels around the entire body; seek immediate veterinary help.

Always make sure an animal has adequate ventilation, shade, and water during hot weather. If you must leave the dog in the car, even for just a few minutes, leave the windows open wide enough to provide circulating air (but not wide enough to allow the dog to escape). Or leave the motor and air conditioner running. The best solution of all in hot weather is to leave the dog at home.

Poisoning

When seeking assistance for the treatment of poisoning, a few simple facts are extremely helpful: *what* the dog ate, *how much* got into his system, and *how long ago* the ingestion occurred. This information will greatly facilitate the veterinarian's plan of action.

You should also keep the number of a local poison control center near the phone at all times. Furthermore, bring any information you have about the substance—the container, label, drug insert, whatever—along with you to the veterinarian.

Lakeland Terrier. *Mary Bloom*

Irish Water Spaniel. *Mary Bloom*   **Silky Terrier.** *Mary Bloom*

Let's look at some of the most common types of poisoning in dogs.

Insecticides (such as flea and tick preparations). The most common signs shown by dogs who are poisoned by these products are trembling, weakness, drooling, vomiting, and loss of bowel control. The situation may be very serious. Immediately remove any flea collar or chemical-containing material from the dog's body or environment, rinse off any dip that might have been applied, and call the veterinarian for advice. Never use more than the recommended amount, strength, or number of products at any one time on your dog.

Rat poison. Rat poison usually contains a powerful anticoagulant that causes its victims to bleed to death. Dogs that accidentally ingest this substance should be induced to vomit immediately, to decrease the chances of the toxin's absorption. They should also be treated with vitamin K injections (plus supportive care as necessary) to boost the ability of their blood to clot.

Other rodenticidal products contain strychnine. This poison is rapidly absorbed, causing convulsions and death within a short time. Immediate induction of vomiting is helpful in the case of strychnine poisoning, but don't waste any time getting to a veterinarian.

Bull Terrier. *The AKC*

Acids, alkalis, and petroleum products. Vomiting is contraindicated in the case of these poisonings, so it's best to consult your veterinarian about any specific treatment. However, here are some general guidelines to help you buy time if assistance is not immediately available.

If the dog has ingested an acidic poison, administer an antacid such as milk of magnesia or Pepto-Bismol. Approximately two teaspoons per five pounds of body weight will help neutralize the acid. To neutralize an alkali substance, give the same dosage of a one part vinegar/four parts water mixture.

In the case of petroleum distillate poisoning, use mineral or vegetable oil to coat the gastrointestinal tract. The dose is one tablespoon per five pounds of body weight.

Antifreeze. Antifreeze, a potent poison thought to taste sweet, is very attractive to animals. Unfortunately, only a tiny amount needs to be ingested before serious kidney damage results. If you suspect that your dog has sampled some of this green liquid, immediately seek veterinary help. There are no measures to take at home. Animal-safe antifreezes are available.

Seizures—Convulsions

The best course of action to take with a dog undergoing a convulsion is to protect him from injuring himself by falling or by striking his head against hard objects. A large blanket or towel may be placed under the dog's head and limbs. Take care when handling the head because the dog may accidentally bite you. There is no need to worry about the dog swallowing his tongue, so don't reach into its mouth.

Seizures vary in length. They are rarely life threatening in themselves but can be very serious if the dog is unable to come out of a convulsion or has multiple seizures with barely a break between them. Factors other than epilepsy can cause seizures. See your veterinarian as soon as possible to try to determine the cause.

Shock

Shock is characterized by collapse of the cardiovascular system. Signs of shock include a rapid, weak heartbeat, dilated pupils, pale gums, and overall weakness; shock demands immediate emergency attention.

Dogs suffer from shock most often as a result of being hit by a car or any other massive injury. It can also occur secondary to serious disease.

Time is precious in treating an animal in shock. Take whatever measures are immediately required, such as controlling hemorrhage, while you transport the dog to an emergency facility. Try to keep the dog as quiet and warm (animals in shock commonly have low body temperature) as possible.

Belgian Tervuren. *Mary Bloom*

Pekingese. *Mary Bloom*

Topical Irritants

Paint, tar, or grease. Never try to remove paint, tar, or grease from a dog's coat with turpentine, gasoline, or other harsh chemicals. These remedies are extremely irritating to the skin and may cause severe reactions. Vegetable oil, on the other hand, works quite well in removing tar and grease from the coat. This may be followed by a cleansing bath using mild dishwashing detergent. The best way to remove paint is to simply (though carefully) cut it away.

Burns. Minor burns are best treated by carefully clipping the hair away from the affected area, cleaning if necessary with a mild soap, and applying a topical antibiotic or steroid ointment. Extensive burns need immediate veterinary care.

Hot spots. Hot spots are focal skin infections that, although not associated with burns, actually feel warm to the touch. They are usually round, red, moist, and painful. Dogs can't seem to stop licking and chewing at the area.

Clip hair away from hot spots, clean thoroughly, and then treat with antibiotic or steroid ointment. If hot spots are severe, dogs are often given oral antibiotics and forced to wear Elizabethan collars—plastic barriers that prevent the dog from reaching the hot spot with its mouth. Hot spots often look very minor at first, but can erupt into large problems if left unattended.

In summary, in a medical emergency, make sure the dog won't bite you, get the dog to a safe place, stabilize the dog, and then get to a veterinarian as soon as possible. And don't forget—if you remain calm in an emergency, your dog will feel more secure.

Bouvier des Flandres. *Mary Bloom*

• 10 •

ALL ABOUT THE AKC

So you have your new dog and you've read this far. Now that you've made the commitment to be a responsible dog owner, we'd love to have you and your dog join us at some of our American Kennel Club events. We're proud of the work we're doing to help dogs and promote responsible dog ownership in our communities. If you want to have a great time with your dog, keep reading to learn about The AKC programs available to you. First, a brief background of The AKC is in order.

Welcome to The AKC

Founded in 1884, The American Kennel Club is the nation's leading not-for-profit organization dedicated to the study, breeding, exhibiting, and advancement of purebred dogs. The AKC's mission statement has three key components, which are (1) to maintain a registry for purebred dogs and preserve its integrity, (2) to sanction dog events that promote interest in, and sustain the process of, breeding for type and function of purebred dogs, and (3) to take whatever actions are necessary to protect and assure the continuation of the sport of purebred dogs. Each of The AKC's many activities supports this mission statement.

Recognized as a world leader in the canine community, The AKC operates the world's largest purebred dog registry. In the year 2000, there were nearly 4,500 American Kennel Club dog clubs. If you wanted to attend a dog event that year, there were 15,000 events (of different types) across the country from which to choose!

The American Kennel Club is a "club of clubs." This means that as an individual person, you cannot join The AKC as a member. The members of The AKC are dog clubs from all over the country, each of which is represented by one voting delegate at The AKC's quarterly meetings. In the year 2000, there were 557 member clubs that had the right to be represented by delegates. These are the clubs that serve as the guardians for individual breeds and specific aspects of the sport.

Conformation Dog Shows

Dog shows, also known as "conformation shows," are the signature events of The American Kennel Club. The word "conformation" relates to the structure or form of something—in this case, a dog. Conformation takes into account the whole picture as well as all of the individual parts.

It would be a terrible mistake to think of a conformation show as a "beauty contest." These shows are serious business. The purpose of conformation shows is to allow breeders an opportunity to exhibit their animals. It is the job of the breeder to preserve and improve the characteristics of individual breeds. Conformation shows provide a forum at which breeding stock can be evaluated by breeding experts.

Kerry Blue Terrier. *The AKC*

Affenpinscher. *Mary Bloom*

All AKC judges are required to demonstrate extensive competency, based upon experience and testing before judging any breed. Judges are also observed at shows by AKC field representatives. When judging conformation, judges look at:

- health, conditioning, and overall appearance
- physical structure and characteristics (such as toplines, coat, shoulder angulations, head shape, and so on)
- temperament
- movement or gait

Within each of these categories, the judge considers how closely each dog matches the Parent Club's written breed Standard. Each breed Standard has specifics regarding the ideal color, size, proportion, and so on. Judges who are judging breeds are familiar with the Standard for each breed.

In 2000, there were 1,716,928 dogs entered in all-breed shows. Dog shows are becoming an increasingly popular sport, so much so that some shows have been featured on television sports channels.

Now that we've told you a little bit about conformation dog shows, the event we are most often known by, let's look at some AKC activities and services that are available to you as a dog owner. For your convenience, the remainder of the topics are listed in alphabetical order.

Canine Health Foundation

The AKC is dedicated to improving the health of purebred dogs. The American Kennel Club's support of the AKC Canine Health Foundation (CHF) shows just how serious that dedication is. The AKC's Canine Health Foundation's mission statement is to "develop resources for basic and applied health programs with an emphasis on canine genetics to improve the quality of life for dogs and their owners."

Ideally, your dog will have a long, happy life. However, sometimes you fall in love with a dog and tragedy strikes. Everything is going along fine when the dog who has become your best buddy suddenly has a seizure. The next thing you know, you are looking for every bit of information you can find on canine epilepsy.

There are an estimated 500 genetic defects in dogs and it is the work of the AKC Canine Health Foundation to fund research that will begin the process to eliminate these genetic disorders. The American Kennel Club is a major financial donor to the foundation.

The CHF also funds the canine genome project. The purpose of this project is to map the genetic code of dogs. This work will eventually allow breeders to determine a dog's genetic health before making decisions about breeding.

Many AKC dog clubs from all over the country have joined the CHF as members and have donated hundreds of thousands of dollars for canine research. It is possible for a person or club interested in a specific breed to make a donation specifically for that breed. For membership on the AKC Canine Health Foundation, visit www.akcchf.org or call 330-995-0807.

Club Relations

We hope you will be excited about participating in AKC events with your dog and you will join one of your local AKC dog clubs. There are clubs for specific breeds, All-Breed clubs for conformation, Field clubs, Obedience Training clubs, Agility clubs, and more.

Komondor. *Mary Bloom*

The Club Relations department of The American Kennel Club keeps track of over 4,500 member, licensed, and sanctioned AKC clubs. Club Relations assists clubs in the AKC membership process (whereby a club becomes a member club of The AKC and has a voting delegate). In the year 2000, 557 member clubs had the right to be represented by delegates. This is the department that helps clubs with bylaw revisions and assists in resolving internal disputes within a club. If you join an AKC club near you, your club might have the opportunity to work with The AKC's Club Relations department. For a list of the AKC clubs nearest you, visit the AKC website at www.akc.org.

Companion Animal Recovery—The "CAR" Program

Accidents happen. A young child accidentally leaves the gate open and the three dogs you love disappear. Little compares to the panic an owner experiences when a dog is missing. AKC Companion Animal Recovery (CAR) is dedicated to providing lifetime recovery services for microchipped and tattooed pets, regardless of species, age, or size. An affiliate organization of The American Kennel Club, CAR reunites lost pets with their owners.

Microchipping is a painless procedure often offered at microchip clinics during major dog shows. You can also ask your veterinarian about microchipping your dog. The microchip used to identify companion animals is about the size of a grain of rice and holds a unique encoded number. People who find lost pets most often contact a veterinarian or animal shelter. Both veterinarians and shelters have scanners that can read microchips. The CAR Program uses the microchip (or tattoo) number to identify the pet and contact the pet's owner.

Membership in CAR provides you with lifetime recovery services 24 hours a day, 365 days a year for your microchipped or tattooed dog. Since CAR began in 1995, more than 55,000 pets have been successfully reunited with their owners. A part of being a responsible dog owner is making sure that your dog has proper identification. To learn more about CAR, visit www.akc.org/love/car or call (800) 252-7894.

Companion Events

Several AKC activities provide the ultimate training for your dog to become a good companion. Four areas including Obedience, Agility, Tracking, and Canine Good Citizen® are grouped together to form the Companion Events Department.

Obedience is a sport that continues to grow. In the year 2000, more than 150,000 dogs competed in AKC obedience. Each year, there is a National Obedience Invitational where the "best of the best" compete over a two-day weekend. At this national event, dogs go through a process of elimination rounds, which ends with one dog winning the National Obedience Championship.

Wirehaired Pointing Griffon. *Mary Bloom*

Irish Terriers. *Mary Bloom*

Agility is one of the fastest growing dog sports. AKC Agility is open to all AKC breeds. The American Kennel Club has the AKC/USA World Agility Championship team, for which the members are selected yearly. The team travels to different countries to represent both The AKC and the United States. If you like fast-paced, exciting, athletic activities, agility may be the sport for you and your dog.

Tracking is the activity for you if your dog is scent-oriented. If your dog isn't scent-oriented, don't worry—there are other activities. If you like being outside and want to train your dog, your dog can learn tracking. Tracking begins with dogs earning the TD title. All breeds can participate in tracking and owners of proficient tracking dogs often get involved in Search and Rescue.

The AKC's Canine Good Citizen® Program is a good foundation for all other training activities. Before your dog shows up at any event, he should demonstrate some basic level of training and good manners. That's what the CGC Program is all about. The beauty of the Canine Good Citizen Program is that this is a program for *every* dog and every dog owner.

Customer Relations

If you have a question about an AKC topic and can't find the answer on The AKC's website, The AKC's Customer Relations division is available to help you.

Whether you are an expert or newcomer to the sport, Customer Service is always ready to answer questions and take orders for products and educational materials. AKC Customer Service handles 70,000 calls per month and hundreds of emails daily. Customer Service can be reached at 919-233-9767.

Scottish Terriers. *Mary Bloom*

DNA

The AKC's DNA Operations Department, part of the Compliance Division, is doing exciting things with DNA technology to aid dogs. DNA, which is short for deoxyribonucleic acid, is the material in cells that contains the genetic code and is responsible for transmitting hereditary instructions. DNA typing (also called DNA profiling or DNA fingerprinting) analyzes and compares DNA samples to determine identity. For example, it can be used to determine paternity or maternity, to positively identify a deceased person, or to determine whether the DNA contained in skin, hair, or blood found at a crime scene came from a certain suspect or witness. DNA analysis is also relevant to the breeding of purebred dogs.

The DNA Operations Department of The AKC uses the same technology employed in human paternity testing to establish the genetic identity of dogs and maintain the integrity of the AKC Stud Book. AKC inspectors visit kennels and collect DNA samples from the sire, dam, and puppies in a litter. Collecting DNA is a simple process that involves using a small bristle brush to swab inside the dog's cheek. Loose cheek cells are deposited on the swab and are the source of DNA for analysis.

When parentage of dogs is found to be erroneous, the DNA Operations Department makes every effort to work with the litter owners to correct the litter registrations. However, if correct parentage cannot be determined, the litter registration must be cancelled. Breeders who refuse inspections are subject to fines and suspensions from AKC privileges.

The AKC also offers DNA Certification on a voluntary basis, and it is required for Frequently Used Sires. To obtain certification, the dog owner collects the DNA sample using the simple cheek swab method, and mails the DNA sample to The AKC with payment. The owner receives an AKC DNA Certificate that shows the dog's DNA profile, and it can be used for parentage verification and genetic identity purposes.

Handlers Program

Dogs can be shown in AKC shows by their owners, friends of owners, or professional handlers. The AKC's new Handlers Program is designed to promote the health and welfare of dogs who are in the care of handlers. The program recognizes handlers who meet The AKC's established criteria and provides a source of guidance to consumers and information on issues pertaining to the handling of dogs.

Skye Terrier. *Mary Bloom*

Bearded Collie. *Mary Bloom*   **Sussex Spaniel.** *Mary Bloom*

Judges Education

The education of judges is an important function of The AKC. American Kennel Club judges are trained at seminars and institutes throughout the country. The AKC produces printed materials and videos for teaching judges about specific breeds. In addition to classroom work, one of the most important parts of a judge's education is the hands-on, real-world training that goes on in the dog show ring or in the field. Judges who are working on approval to judge a new breed will sometimes be seen observing with an experienced judge. AKC judges are involved in ongoing education that takes place in the classroom, in the dog show ring, and in the settings in which specific breeds work, coupled with extensive experience in the sport prior to applying to judge.

Junior Showmanship

At The AKC, we recognize that young people are the future of our sport. Junior Showmanship Classes have been in existence for more than seventy years. In 1997, The American Kennel Club established the National Junior Organization (NJO) to encourage handling skills and good sportsmanship in young people between the ages of 10 and 18. The National Junior Organization recognizes juniors (no minimum age and up to age 18) for handling a dog to an AKC title in *any* AKC event.

The AKC awards Junior Showmanship scholarships, which are based on commitment to the sport of dogs, outstanding academic achievement, and financial need. Seminars and educational events for Juniors are held at various AKC dog shows around the country. At these seminars, Juniors receive training by AKC staff and judges, professional handlers, and other canine experts, such as veterinarians. Many Juniors and their dogs participate in the various AKC Performance activities.

In the United States, there are more than 11,000 Junior handlers who participate in the Juniors program. Some of these Juniors will go on to pursue careers in dogs as professional handlers, breeders, or veterinarians.

Even when Juniors become adults and don't stay involved in exhibiting dogs, Junior Showmanship teaches valuable lessons that will last a lifetime. When a sport has the power to teach a young person lessons such as good sportsmanship, grace in victory, dignity in defeat, tenacity and perseverance, and how to put an animal's needs above your own, the result is that everybody is a winner.

A Junior may obtain a number for tracking participation in AKC events by calling 919-816-3814 or emailing juniors@akc.org

Legislation

To protect the interests of dogs and dog owners, the AKC Canine Legislation deals with legislative issues pertaining to dogs. Among them are legislation discriminating against specific breeds; unreasonable breeding restrictions or extreme licensing fees; limits on pet ownership and access to public parks; consumer protection laws for puppy buyers; and protecting field trials on federally funded hunting lands. AKC Canine Legislation develops materials and serves as a resource to dog fanciers who are addressing legislative concerns in their local areas. If you need assistance with implementing a program in your community (such as establishing a dog park), check our Canine Legislation materials on this topic.

Library

The American Kennel Club's library, housed at AKC Headquarters in New York City, is not a lending library. This is a library collection and if you love dogs, you owe it to yourself to visit the library at least once. More than 17,000 volumes make up one of the most impressive dog book collections in the world. There are 2,500 rare books, periodicals, stud books from other countries, stamps, bookplates, and videos. If you spend an afternoon in the AKC Library, there's a good chance you'll be in the company of scholars and writers who are busy with canine research. The AKC Library has some of the most important historical works on dogs in any collection and the library staff can help you find anything you need. To contact the AKC Library, phone 212-696-8245.

Museum

The American Kennel Club Museum of the Dog is housed in St. Louis, Missouri. This museum holds one of the largest collections of dog-related fine art in the world. The AKC supports the museum by providing an annual operating grant. The AKC also provides additional funding for the restoration of artwork and facility repairs. The AKC Museum of the Dog is open to the public year round. For information, call 314-821-3647.

Performance Events

Mentioned in detail in an earlier chapter, the Performance Events are very important as they demonstrate the dog's ability to perform the functions for which it was bred. Performance Events include Field Trials, Hunt Tests, Lure Coursing, Herding, Earthdog, and Coonhound Events.

The popularity of AKC Performance Events is increasing and a number of national events have been televised. Few people realize there are actually more Performance Events per year than Conformation Events. In the year 2000, there were nearly 4,800 AKC-licensed Performance Events.

Publications

The American Kennel Club has several publications that can enhance your knowledge about dogs and dog events. In print for more than 100 years, the *AKC Gazette* is a monthly all-breed magazine. You can purchase the monthly *AKC Gazette* at some bookstores, or you can take advantage of reduced prices if you subscribe to the magazine. The *AKC Gazette* includes articles every month on a variety of topics related to all aspects of dogs. The *Events Calendar* is a supplement to the *AKC Gazette*. This calendar provides a listing of dog events all over the country, the dates of the events, and entry information.

If your new dog is a puppy registered with The American Kennel Club, you should have received *AKC puppies*. This informative magazine is sent to all dog registrants and it reaches more than one million readers each year.

Field Spaniel. *Audrey Pavia*

Public Education

The AKC's Public Education division works with the owner at the other end of the dog's leash. The goal of AKC Public Education is to teach about responsible dog ownership and the joys of participating in AKC events to members of the general public, dog owners, educators, and legislators.

AKC Public Education administers the Canine Ambassador Program. More than 1,000 volunteers from AKC affiliated clubs who are "Canine Ambassadors" visit schools and youth programs (often with their dogs) to teach about purebred dogs, responsible dog ownership, and safety around dogs.

In addition to the Canine Ambassadors, AKC Public Education organizes and provides support services to 3,000 Public Education Coordinators (PECs) around the country. PECs are volunteer dog club members who promote the sport of dogs in their communities.

Also operating within the Public Education and Canine Legislation Department is Club Educational Services. If you attend one of the AKC dog shows that includes the AKC Informational Booth, you will meet some of our Club Educational Services staff. The AKC Booth reaches more than 80,000 people every year at shows. If you see the AKC booth at a show, stop by, say hello, and take advantage of AKC printed materials, videos, products, and website demonstrations.

Bedlington Terrier. *Mary Bloom*   **Staffordshire Bull Terrier.** *Mary Bloom*

Website: www.akc.org

As a dog owner, we think you'll find that the AKC website puts just about every piece of useful dog related information at your fingertips. All you need is access to a computer and you can let your fingers do the walking. The AKC's Information Services division, among many other functions, maintains The AKC's website. The AKC website has nearly one million visitors per month and has been described as the most popular dog-related address on the Internet.

You can use The AKC's website to access the TopDogs reports. These reports provide information on show records and rankings for every dog who has participated in competitive events. The web will teach you what you need to know about specific breeds. You'll get the latest updates on AKC programs and you'll be able to read the highlights from shows around the country. You can shop at The AKC's Online Store to find the latest in AKC materials and products. And just think, the time you save with this efficient method of shopping and gathering information can be used to train your dog!

We hope that you've found the information we've provided in *The American Kennel Club Dog Care and Training*, Second Edition, useful and that it has helped you and your dog get off to a good start. If we can help in any way as you continue to learn about dogs and enjoy your canine companion, please contact us. We're here to help. We're looking forward to meeting you and your dog at an AKC event soon.

THE DOG'S EXTERNAL AND SKELETAL ANATOMY

On the seven pages that follow we present a series of magnificent drawings by Mr. Stephen J. Hubbell, a celebrated artist and dog show judge. These clearly demonstrate what a wonderful work of design the dog's body truly is. Study these carefully and you will develop a deeper appreciation of your dog and its capacity to function so well in such an amazing variety of ways.

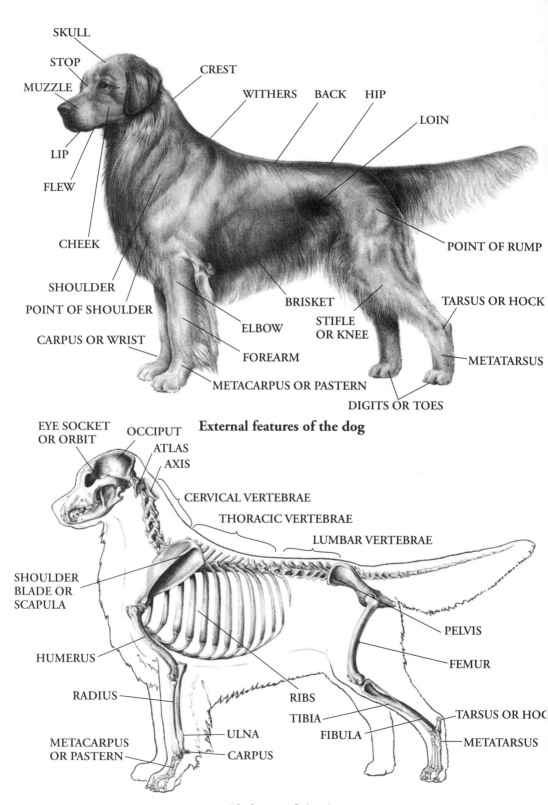

SKULL

STOP

MUZZLE

CREST

WITHERS BACK HIP

LOIN

LIP

FLEW

POINT OF RUMP

CHEEK

SHOULDER

POINT OF SHOULDER

CARPUS OR WRIST

BRISKET

ELBOW

STIFLE
OR KNEE

TARSUS OR HOCK

METATARSUS

FOREARM

METACARPUS OR PASTERN

DIGITS OR TOES

External features of the dog

EYE SOCKET
OR ORBIT

OCCIPUT

ATLAS

AXIS

CERVICAL VERTEBRAE

THORACIC VERTEBRAE

LUMBAR VERTEBRAE

SHOULDER
BLADE OR
SCAPULA

PELVIS

HUMERUS

FEMUR

RADIUS

RIBS

TIBIA

TARSUS OR HOC

ULNA

FIBULA

METATARSUS

METACARPUS
OR PASTERN

CARPUS

Skeleton of the dog

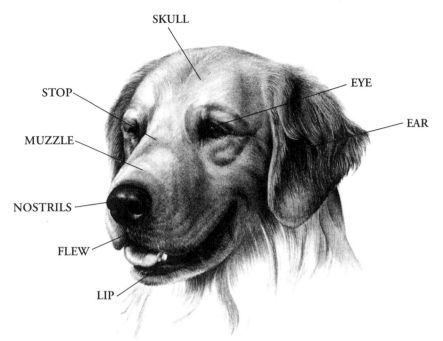

SKULL

EYE

STOP

EAR

MUZZLE

NOSTRILS

FLEW

LIP

External features of the dog's head

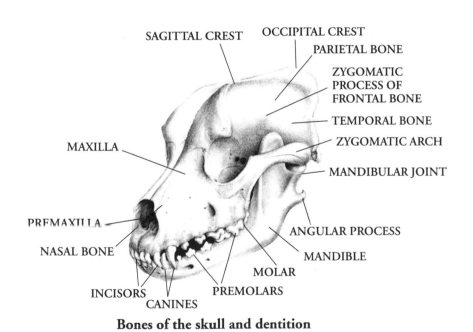

SAGITTAL CREST

OCCIPITAL CREST

PARIETAL BONE

ZYGOMATIC PROCESS OF FRONTAL BONE

TEMPORAL BONE

ZYGOMATIC ARCH

MAXILLA

MANDIBULAR JOINT

PREMAXILLA

ANGULAR PROCESS

NASAL BONE

MANDIBLE

MOLAR

INCISORS

PREMOLARS

CANINES

Bones of the skull and dentition

ALMOND

OVAL

FULL, ROUND, GLOBULAR

TRIANGULAR

Eye types

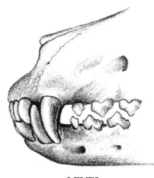
LEVEL

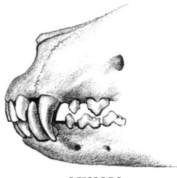
SCISSORS

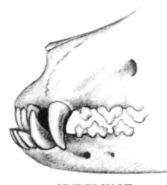
UNDERSHOT

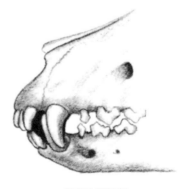
OVERSHOT

Bites

NORMAL STRAIGHT

TOO NARROW IN FRONT
AND EAST-WEST FEET

CHIPPENDALE OR
FIDDLE FRONT

OUT AT ELBOW AND
TOO WIDE IN FRONT

STRAIGHT FORWARD

KNUCKLED OVER

DOWN IN PASTERN

Fronts

PADS

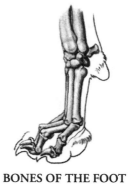

BONES OF THE FOOT

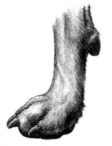

ROUND OR CAT FOOT

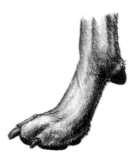

HARE FOOT

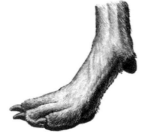

FLAT FOOT OR
DOWN IN PASTERN

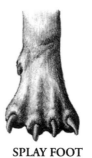

SPLAY FOOT

Feet

CORRECT, STRAIGHT, NORMAL

COW-HOCKED

BANDY OR WIDE

NARROW

NORMAL ANGULATED
HINDQUARTERS

STRAIGHT STIFLES

Rears

PLUME

GAY

CURLED

DOUBLE CURL

SICKLE

OTTER

WHIP

RING AT END

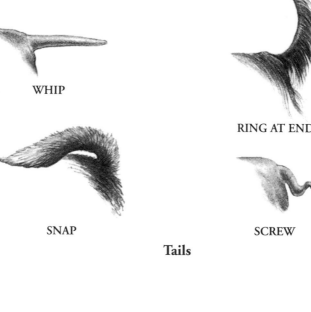

SNAP

SCREW

Tails

APPENDIX I: CLUBS

No matter what your interest in dogs, chances are good that there's a dog club nearby where you can meet people who share your interests. At latest count in early 2001, there were more than 4,500 different dog clubs in the United States that hold events under AKC Rules and Regulations. The odds are there's a club near you.

The AKC recognizes 13 different types of clubs:

- All-Breed Clubs
- Group Clubs
- Specialty (Parent) Clubs
- Specialty (Local Breed) Clubs
- Obedience Clubs
- Tracking Clubs
- Field Trial Clubs
- Hunting Test Clubs
- Herding Clubs
- Lure Coursing Clubs
- Agility Clubs
- Earthdog Clubs
- Coonhound Clubs

The largest group of clubs is the specialty or breed clubs. There are more than 2,100 specialty clubs in the United States. There are two types of specialty clubs. The first is the national (or parent) breed club; for example, the Golden Retriever Club of America. The AKC recognizes only one club as the national or parent breed club for each recognized breed. The second type of specialty (breed) club is the local specialty; for example, the Golden Retriever Club of Greater Los Angeles or the Kansas City Golden Retriever Club.

It is this extensive network of serious fanciers of the respective breeds that you should contact to help you choose your dog. You may obtain detailed information about the clubs nearest you by contacting AKC Customer Service, 580 Centerview Drive, Raleigh, NC 27606; phone 919-233-9767.

APPENDIX II: TITLES AND ABBREVIATIONS

Dogs compete in the various competitions offered under the Rules and Regulations of The American Kennel Club for different titles. When a dog completes the requirements for one of the titles, official note of the title is made on the dog's AKC records. Thereafter, the notation of title will always appear with the dog's name in The AKC's records. Some titles are indicated before the dog's name (prefixes), and some appear after the dog's name (suffixes). The titles and their abbreviations are as follows:

Prefixes

Conformation

Ch.—Champion

Obedience

NOC—National Obedience Champion
OTCH—Obedience Trial Champion
VCCH—Versatile Companion Champion

Tracking

CT—Champion Tracker (TD, TDX, and VST)

Agility

MACH—Master Agility Champion
MACH2, MACH3, MACH4, and so on. MACH may be followed by a number designation to indicate the quantity of times the dog has met the requirements of the MACH title.

Field Trials

FC—Field Champion
AFC—Amateur Field Champion
NFC—National Field Champion
NAFC—National Amateur Field Champion
NOGDC—National Gun Dog Champion

Herding

HC—Herding Champion

Dual

DC—Dual Champion (Ch. and FC)

Trial

TC—Triple Champion (Ch., FC, and OTCH)

Coonhounds

NCH—Nite Champion
GNCH—Grand Nite Champion
SHNCH—Senior Grand Nite Champion
GCH—Senior Champion
SGCH—Senior Grand Champion
GFC—Grand Field Champion
SGFC—Senior Grand Field Champion
WCH—Water Race Champion
GWCH—Water Race Grand Champion
SGWCH—Senior Grand Water Race Champion

Suffixes

Obedience

CD—Companion Dog
CDX   Companion Dog Excellent
UD—Utility Dog
UDX—Utility Dog Excellent
VCD1—Versatile Companion Dog 1
VCD2—Versatile Companion Dog 2
VCD3—Versatile Companion Dog 3
VCD4—Versatile Companion Dog 4

Lure Coursing

JC—Junior Courser
SC—Senior Courser
MC—Master Courser

Tracking

TD—Tracking Dog
TDX—Tracking Dog Excellent
VST—Variable Surface Tracker

Agility

NA—Novice Agility
OA—Open Agility
AX—Agility Excellent
MX—Master Agility Excellent
NAJ—Novice Jumpers with Weaves
OAJ—Open Jumpers with Weaves
AXJ—Excellent Jumpers with Weaves
MXJ—Master Excellent Jumpers with Weaves

Hunting Test

JH—Junior Hunter
SH—Senior Hunter
MH—Master Hunter

Herding Test

HT—Herding Tested
PT—Pre-Trial Tested
HSAdsc—Herding Started Course A (ducks, sheep, cattle)
HIAdsc—Herding Intermediate Course A (ducks, sheep, cattle)
HXAdsc—Herding Advanced Course A (ducks, sheep, cattle)
HSBdsc—Herding Started Course B (ducks, sheep, cattle)
HIBdsc—Herding Intermediate Course B (ducks, sheep, cattle)
HXBdsc—Herding Advanced Course B (ducks, sheep, cattle)
HSCs—Herding Started Course C (sheep)
HICs—Herding Intermediate Course C (sheep)
HXCs—Herding Advanced Course C (sheep)

Lure Coursing

JC—Junior Courser
SC—Senior Courser
MC—Master Courser

Earthdog

JE—Junior Earthdog
SE—Senior Earthdog
ME—Master Earthdog

GLOSSARY

Abdomen: The portion of the dog's body between the chest and the hindquarters.

Action: Any performance of function or movement, either of any part or organ, or of the whole body. Used as a synonym for gait in some standards.

AKC, The: The American Kennel Club.

Albino: Animal deficient in pigmentation.

Almond eyes: The eye set in surrounding tissue of almond shape.

Angulation: The angles formed by a meeting of the bones; mainly, the shoulder, upper arm, stifle, and hock.

Arm: The anatomical region between the shoulder and elbow joints, consisting of the humerus and associated muscles. Sometimes referred to as "upper arm."

Back: Variable in meaning depending upon context of the standard. In some standards defined as the vertebrae between the withers and the loin.

Bad mouth: Crooked or unaligned teeth; bite overshot or undershot in excess of standard specifications.

Balanced: A consistent whole; symmetrical, typically proportioned as a whole or as regards its separate parts; i.e., balance of head, balance of body, or balance of head and body.

Bandy legs: Having a bend of leg outward.

Barrel: Rounded rib section.

Bay: The prolonged bark or voice of the hunting hound.

Beady eyes: Small, round, and glittering, imparting an expression foreign to the breed.

Beard: Thick, long hair growth on the underjaw.

Beefy: Overheavy development of the hindquarters.

Belly: The underline of the abdomen.

Bench show: A dog show at which the dogs competing for prizes are "benched" or leashed on benches.

Best in show: A dog-show award to the dog judged best of all breeds.

Bird dog: A sporting dog trained to hunt birds.

Bitch: A female dog.

Bite: The relative position of the upper and lower teeth when the mouth is closed. *See* Level bite, Overshot, Scissors bite, Undershot.

Blaze: A white stripe running up the center of the face, usually between the eyes.

Blocky: Square or cubelike formation of the head.

Bloom: The sheen of a coat in prime condition.

Board: To feed, house, and care for a dog for a fee.

Bodied up: Mature, well-developed.

Body: The anatomical section between the forequarters and the hindquarters.

Body length: Distance from the point of the shoulder to the rearmost projection of the upper thigh (point of the buttocks).

Bone: The relative size (girth) of a dog's leg bones. Substance.

Bossy: Overdevelopment of the shoulder muscles.

Break: Term used to describe changing of coat color from puppies to adult stages.

Breastbone: Bone in forepart of chest.

Breed: Purebred dogs more or less uniform in size and structure, as produced and maintained by humans.

Breeder: A person who breeds dogs. Under AKC rules, the breeder of a dog is the owner (or, if the dam was leased, the lessee) of the dam of the dog when the dam was bred.

Breeding particulars: Sire, dam, date of birth, sex, color, etc.

Brick-shaped: Rectangular.

Brindle: A fine, even mixture of black hairs with hairs of a lighter color, usually tan, brown, or gray.

Brisket: The forepart of the body below the chest, between the forelegs, closest to the ribs.

Broken color: Self color broken by white or another color.

Broken-haired: A roughed-up wire coat.

Broken-up face: A receding nose, together with a deep stop, wrinkle, and undershot jaw. (Bulldog, Pekingese.)

Brood bitch: A female used for breeding. Brood matron.

Brows: The ridges formed above the eyes by frontal bone contours. (Superciliary arches.)

Brush: A bushy tail; a tail heavy with hair.

Brushing: A gaiting fault, when parallel pasterns are so close that the legs "brush" in passing.

Bull neck: A heavy neck, well-muscled.

Burr: The inside of the ear; i.e., the irregular formation visible within the cup.

Butterfly nose: A parti-colored nose; i.e., dark, spotted with flesh color.

Buttocks: The rump or hips.

Button ear: The ear flap folding forward, the tip lying close to the skull so as to cover the orifice, and pointing toward the eye.

Camel back: Arched back, like that of a one-hump camel.

Canine: A group of animals—dogs, foxes, wolves, jackals.

Canines: The two upper and two lower sharp-pointed teeth next to the incisors. Fangs.

Cape: Profuse hair enveloping the shoulder region.

Carpals: Bones of the pastern joints.

Castrate: To remove the testicles of the male dog.

Cat foot: Round, compact foot, with well-arched toes, tightly bunched or close-cupped.

CD (Companion Dog):   A suffix used with the name of a dog that has been recorded a Companion Dog by The AKC as a result of having won certain minimum scores in Novice Classes at a specified number of AKC licensed or member obedience trials.

CDX (Companion Dog Excellent):   A suffix used with the name of a dog that has been recorded a Companion Dog Excellent by The AKC as a result of having won certain minimum scores in Open Classes at a specified number of AKC licensed or member obedience trials.

Champion (Ch.):   A prefix used with the name of a dog that has been recorded a Champion by The AKC as a result of defeating a specified number of dogs in specified competition at a series of AKC licensed or member dog shows.

Character: Expression, individuality, and general appearance and deportment as considered typical of a breed.

Cheeky: Cheeks prominently rounded; thick, protruding.

Chest: The part of the body or trunk that is enclosed by the ribs.

China eye: A clear blue eye.

Chippendale front: Named after the Chippendale chair. Forelegs out at elbows, pasterns close, and feet turned out. *See* Fiddle front, French front.

Chiseled: Clean-cut in head, particularly beneath the eyes.

Choke collar: A leather or chain collar fitted to the dog's neck in such a manner that the degree of tension exerted by the hand tightens or loosens it.

Chops: Jowls or pendulous flesh of the lips and jaw. (Bulldog.)

Chorea: A nervous jerking caused by involuntary contraction of the muscles, usually affecting the face or legs.

Clip: The method of trimming the coat in some breeds, notably the Poodle.

Clipping: When pertaining to gait, the back foot striking the front foot.

Cloddy: Low, thickset, comparatively heavy.

Close-coupled: Comparatively short from withers to hipbones.

Coarse: Lacking refinement.

Coat: The dog's hair covering. Most breeds possess two coats: an outercoat and an undercoat.

Cobby: Short-bodied, compact.

Collar: The marking around the neck, usually white. Also a leather or chain for restraining or leading the dog, when the leash is attached.

Compact: Term used to describe the firmly joined union of various body parts. Also to describe a short- to medium-length coat, very close-lying, with a dense undercoat and giving a smooth outline.

Condition: Health as shown by the coat, state of flesh, general appearance, and deportment.

Conformation: The form and structure, make and shape; arrangement of the parts in conformance with breed-standard demands.

Congenital: An inherited feature present at birth.

Coupling: The part of the body between the ribs and pelvis; the loin.

Covering ground: The ratio of the distance between the ground and brisket, and the distance between front and rear legs. As in "covers too much ground."

Cow-hocked: When the hocks turn toward each other.

Crank tail: A tail carried down and resembling a crank in shape.

Crest: The upper, arched portion of the neck.

Cropping: The cutting or trimming of the ear leather for the purpose of inducing the ears to stand erect.

Crossbred: A dog whose sire and dam are representatives of two different breeds.

Croup: The back part of the back, above the hind legs.

Crown: The highest part of the head; the topskull.

Cryptorchid: The adult whose testicles are abnormally retained in the abdominal cavity. Bilateral cryptorchidism involves both sides; that is, neither testicle has descended into the scrotum. Unilateral cryptorchidism involves one side only; that is, one testicle is retained or hidden, and one descended.

Cur: A mongrel.

Cushion: Fullness or thickness of the upper lips.

Cynology: The study of canines.

Dam: The female parent.

Deciduous: Not permanent, but cast off at maturity. Used in reference to baby or milk teeth.

Dentition: Reference to the number of teeth characteristic of a species, and to their arrangement in the jaws.

Depth of chest: Measured from the withers to the lowest point of the sternum.

Dewclaw: An extra claw or functionless digit on the inside of the leg; a rudimentary fifth toe.

Dewlap: Loose, pendulous skin under the throat.

Disqualification: A decision made by a judge or by a bench show committee following a determination that a dog has a condition that makes it ineligible for any further competition under the dog show rules or under the standard for its breed.

Distemper teeth: Teeth discolored or pitted as result of distemper or other enervating disease or deficiency.

Dock: To shorten the tail by cutting.

Dog: A male dog; also used collectively to designate both male and female.

Dog show: A competitive exhibition standard of perfection for each breed.

Dog Show, Conformation (Licensed): An event held under AKC rules at which championship points are awarded. May be for all breeds, or for a single breed (Specialty Show).

Domed: Evenly rounded in topskull; convex instead of flat. Domy.

Double coat: An outer coat resistant to weather and protective against brush and brambles, together with an undercoat of softer hair for warmth and waterproofing.

Down-faced: The muzzle inclining downwards from the skull to the tip of the nose.

Down in pastern: Weak or faulty pastern (metacarpus) set at a pronounced angle from the vertical.

Drive: A solid thrusting of the hindquarters, denoting sound locomotion.

Drop ear: The ends of the ear folded or drooping forward, as contrasted with erect or prick ears.

Dry neck: The skin taut; neither loose nor wrinkled.

Dual champion: A dog that has won both a bench show and a field trial championship.

Dudley nose: Flesh-colored.

East-West front: Incorrectly positioned pasterns that cause the feet to turn outward. Usually associated with a narrow front.

Elbow: The joint between the upper arm and the forearm.

Elbows out: Turning out or off from the body; not held close.

Entire: A dog whose reproductive system is complete.

Even bite: Meeting of front teeth at edges with no overlap of upper or lower teeth.

Ewe neck: Concave curvature of the top neckline.

Expression: The general appearance of all features of the head as viewed from the front and as typical of the breed.

Eyeteeth: The upper canines.

Fall: Hair overhanging the face.

Fallow: Pale cream to light fawn color; pale; pale yellow; yellow-red.

Fancier: A person especially interested and usually active in some phase of the sport of purebred dogs.

Fangs: *See* Canines.

Fawn: A brownish red-yellow with hue of medium brilliance.

Femur: Thigh bone. Extends from hip to stifle.

Fetch: The retrieve of game by the dog; also the command to do so.

Fibula: The outer and smaller of the two bones of the lower thigh.

Fiddle front: Forelegs out at elbows, pasterns close, and feet turned out. French front.

Field Champion (Field Ch.): A prefix used with the name of a dog recorded a Field Champion by The AKC as a result of defeating a specified number of dogs in specified competition at a series of AKC licensed or member field trials.

Field Trial: A competition for certain Hound or Sporting Breeds in which dogs are judged on ability and style in finding or retrieving game or following a game trial.

Filled-up face: Smooth facial contours, free of excessive muscular development.

Flag: A long tail carried high; usually referring to one of the Pointing breeds.

Flank: The side of the body between the last rib and the hip.

Flat bone: The leg bone whose girth is elliptical rather than round.

Flat-sided: Ribs insufficiently rounded as they approach the sternum or breastbone.

Flat withers: A fault that is the result of short upright shoulder blades that unattractively join the withers abruptly.

Flews: Upper lips pendulous, particularly at their inner corners.

Floating rib: The last, or thirteenth rib, which is unattached to other ribs.

Flush: To drive birds from cover, to force them to take flight. To spring.

Flying ears: Any characteristic drop ears or semi-prick ears that stand or "fly."

Forearm: The bone of the forelegs between the elbow and the pastern.

Foreface: The front part of the head, before the eyes. Muzzle.

Forequarters: The combined front assembly from its uppermost component, the shoulder blade, down to the feet.

Foster mother: A bitch or other animal, such as a cat, used to nurse whelps not her own.

Foxy: Sharp expression; pointed nose with short foreface.

French front: *See* Fiddle front.

Front: The forepart of the body as viewed head on; i.e., forelegs, chest, brisket, and shoulder line.

Frontal bone: The skull bone over the eyes.

Furnishings: The long hair on the foreface of certain breeds.

Furrow: A slight indentation or median line down the center of the skull to the stop.

Gait: The pattern of footsteps at various rates of speed, each pattern distinguished by a particular rhythm and footfall. The two gaits acceptable in the show ring are walk and trot.

Gay tail: The tail carried up.

Genealogy: Recorded family descent.

Goose neck: An elongated, tubular-shaped neck. Also termed swan neck.

Goose rump: Too steep or sloping a croup.

Grizzle: Bluish-gray color.

Groom: To brush, comb, trim, or otherwise make a dog's coat neat.

Groups: The breeds as grouped in seven divisions to facilitate judging.

Guard hairs: The longer, smoother, stiffer hairs that grow through the undercoat and normally conceal it.

Gun dog: A dog trained to work with his master in finding live game and retrieving game that has been shot.

Hackles: Hair on neck and back raised involuntarily in fright or anger.

Hallmark: A distinguishing characteristic, such as the spectacles of the Keeshond.

Ham: Muscular development of the hind leg just above the stifle.

Handler: A person who handles a dog in the show ring or at a field trial.

Hare foot: Foot in which the two center digits appear appreciably longer than the outside and inside toes of the foot, and the arching of the toes is less marked, making the foot appear longer overall.

Harness: A leather strap shaped around the shoulders and chest, with a ring at its top over the withers.

Haw: A third eyelid or membrane in the inside corner of the eye.

Head planes: Viewed in profile, the contours of the top skull from occiput to stop, and of the foreface from stop to tip of nose. Usually spoken of in relation to one another.

Heat: Seasonal period of the female. Estrus.

Heel: *See* Hock; also a command to the dog to keep close beside its handler.

Height: Vertical measurement from the withers to the ground; usually referred to as shoulder height. *See* Withers.

High standing: Tall and upstanding, with plenty of leg.

Hindquarters: Rear assembly of dog (pelvis, thighs, hocks, and paws).

Hock: The tarsus or collection of bones of the hind leg forming the joint between the second thigh and the metatarsus; the dog's true heel.

Hocks well let down: Hock joints close to the ground.

Hound: A dog commonly used for hunting by scent or sight.

Hound-marked: A coloration composed of white, tan, and black. The ground color, usually white, may be marked with tan and/or black patches on the head, back, legs, and tail. The extent and the exact location of such markings, however, differ in breeds and individuals.

Inbreeding: The mating of closely related dogs of the same standard breed.

Incisors: The six upper and six lower front teeth between the canines. Their point of contact forms the "bite."

In-shoulder: Shoulders point in, not parallel with, backbone, a fault found in dogs with shoulder blades too far forward on chest.

Interbreeding: The breeding together of dogs of different breeds.

Iris: The colored membrane surrounding the pupil of the eye.

Isabella: Fawn or light bay color.

Jowls: Flesh of lips and jaws.

Judge: The arbiter in the dog show ring, obedience trial, or field trial.

Keel: The rounded outline of the lower chest, between the prosternum and end of the breastbone.

Kennel: Building or enclosure where dogs are kept.

Kink tail: The tail sharply bent.

Kiss marks: Tan spots on the cheeks and over the eyes.

Knee joint: Stifle joint.

Knuckling over: Faulty structure of carpus (wrist) joint allowing it to double forward under the weight of the standing dog; double-jointed wrist, often with slight swelling of the bones.

Layback: The angle of the shoulder blade as compared with the vertical.

Lead: A strap, cord, or chain attached to the collar or harness for the purpose of restraining or leading the dog. Leash.

Leather: The flap of the ear.

Level bite: When the front teeth (incisors) of the upper and lower jaws meet exactly edge to edge. Pincer bite.

Level gait: Dog moves without rise or fall of withers.

Line breeding: The mating of related dogs of the same standard breed, within the line or family, to a common ancestor, as, for example, a dog to his granddam or a bitch to her grandsire.

Lippy: Pendulous lips or lips that do not fit tightly.

Litter: The puppy or puppies of one whelping.

Liver: A color; deep, reddish brown.

Loaded shoulders: When the shoulder blades are shoved out from the body by overdevelopment of the muscles.

Loin: Region of the body on either side of the vertebral column between the last ribs and the hindquarters.

Loose slung: Construction in which the attachment of the body at the shoulders is looser than desirable.

Lower thigh: *See* Second thigh.

Lumber: Superfluous flesh.

Lumbering: An awkward gait.

Mane: Long and profuse hair on top and sides of the neck.

Mask: Dark shading on the foreface. (Mastiff, Boxer, Pekingese.)

Match show: Usually an informal dog show at which no championship points are awarded.

Mate: To breed a dog and bitch.

Median line: *See* Furrow.

Metatarsus: Rear pastern.

Milk teeth: First teeth.

Miscellaneous Class: A competitive class at dog shows for dogs of certain specified breeds for which no regular dog show classification is provided.

Mismarks: Self colors with any area of white on back between withers and tail, on sides between elbows and back of hindquarters, or on ears. Black with white markings and no tan present. (Pembroke Welsh Corgi.)

Molars: Dog has four premolars on each side of the upper and lower jaw. There are two true molars on each side of the upper jaw, and three on each side of the lower jaw. Upper molars have three roots, lower molars have two roots.

Molera: Incomplete, imperfect, or abnormal ossification of the skull.

Mongrel: A dog whose parents are of two different breeds.

Monorchid: A unilateral cryptorchid. *See* Cryptorchid.

Moving close: When the hocks turn in and pasterns drop straight to the ground and move parallel to one another, the dog is "moving close" in the rear. Action places severe strain on ligaments and muscles.

Moving straight: Term descriptive of balanced gaiting in which angle of inclination begins at the shoulder or hip joint, and limbs remain relatively straight from these points to the pads of the feet, even as the legs flex or extend in reaching or thrusting.

Muzzle: The head in front of the eyes—nasal bone, nostrils, and jaws. Foreface. Also, a strap or wire cage attached to the foreface to prevent the dog from biting or from picking up food.

Muzzle band: White marking around the muzzle.

Neck well set-on: Good neckline, merging gradually with strong withers, forming a pleasing transition into topline.

Nick: A breeding that produces desirable puppies.

Nose: Organ of smell; also, the ability to detect by means of scent.

Obedience Trial (Licensed): An event held under AKC rules at which a "leg" toward an obedience degree can be earned.

Obedience Trial Champion (OTCH): A prefix used with the names of a dog that has been recorded an Obedience Trial Champion by the The AKC as the result of having won the number of points and First Place wins specified in the current Obedience Regulations.

Obliquely placed eyes: Eyes with outer corner higher up in the skull than their inner ones. Requested in Alaskan Malamute and Bull Terrier standards.

Oblique shoulders: Shoulders well laid back. The ideal shoulder should slant at 45 degrees to the grounds, forming an approximate right angle with the humerus at the shoulder joint.

Occiput: Upper, back point of the skull.

Occipital protuberance: A prominently raised occiput characteristic of some gun-dog breeds.

Open bitch: A bitch that can be bred.

Open Class: A class at dog shows in which all dogs of a breed, champions and imported dogs included, may compete.

Otter tail: Thick at the root, round, and tapering, with the hair parted or divided on the underside.

Out at elbows: Elbows turning out from the body as opposed to being held close.

Out at shoulder: With shoulder blades loosely attached to the body, leaving the shoulders jutting out in relief and increasing the breadth of the front.

Out at walk: To lease or lend a puppy to someone for raising.

Outcrossing: The mating of unrelated individuals of the same breed.

Oval chest: Chest deeper than wide.

Overhang: A heave or pronounced brow. (Pekingese.)

Overreaching: Fault in the trot caused by more angulation and drive from behind than in front, so that the rear feet are forced to stop to one side of the forefeet to avoid interfering or clipping.

Overshot: The front teeth (incisors) of the upper jaw overlap and do not touch the front teeth of the lower jaw when the mouth is closed.

Pads: Tough, shock-absorbing projections on the underside of the feet. Soles.

Paper foot: A flat foot with thin pads.

Parent club: National club for the breed. Listing with name and address of secretary can be obtained from The American Kennel Club, 260 Madison Avenue, New York, NY 10016.

Parti-color: Variegated in patches of two or more colors.

Pastern: Commonly recognized as the region of the foreleg between the carpus or wrist and the digits.

Pedigree: The written record of a dog's descent of three generations or more.

Pelvis: Hip bone.

Pied: Comparatively large patches of two or more colors. Piebald, parti-colored.

Pigeon-breast: A chest with a short protruding breastbone.

Pigeon-toed: Toes pointing in.

Pig Eyes: Eyes set too close.

Pile: Dense undercoat of soft hair.

Plume: A long fringe of hair hanging from the tail, as in Setters.

Point: The immovable stance of the hunting dog taken to indicate the presence and position of game.

Points: Color on face, ears, legs, and tail when correlated—usually white, black, or tan.

Police dog: Any dog trained for police work.

Prick ear: Carried erect and usually pointed at the tip.

Professional handler: A person who shows dogs for a fee.

Pump handle: Long tail, carried high.

Puppy: A dog under 12 months of age.

Purebred: A dog whose sire and dam belong to the same breed, and are themselves of unmixed descent since recognition of the breed.

Quality: Refinement, fineness.

Racy: Tall, of comparatively slight build.

Rangy: Long-bodied, usually lacking depth in chest.

Rat tail: The root thick and covered with soft curls; at the tip devoid of hair, or having the appearance of being clipped.

Reach of front: Length of forward stride taken by forelegs without wasted or excessive motion.

Register: To record with The AKC a dog's breeding particulars.

Retrieve: A hunting term. The act of bringing back shot game to the handler.

Ribbed up: Long ribs that angle back from the spinal column (45 degrees is ideal); last rib is long.

Ring tail: Carried up and around almost in a circle.

Roach back: A convex curvature of the back toward the loin.

Rocking horse: Both front and rear legs extended out from body as in an old-fashioned rocking horse.

Roman nose: A nose whose bridge is so comparatively high as to form a slightly convex line from forehead to nose tip. Ram's nose.

Rose ear: A small drop ear that folds over and back so as to reveal the burr.

Rudder: The tail.

Ruff: Thick, longer hair growth around the neck.

Saber tail: Carried in a semicircle.

Sable: A lacing of black hairs over a lighter ground color. In Collies and Shetland Sheepdogs, a brown color ranging from golden to mahogany.

Saddle back: Overlong back, with a dip behind the withers.

Scissors bite: A bite in which the outer side of the lower incisors touches the inner side of the upper incisors.

Screw tail: A naturally short tail twisted in more or less spiral formation.

Second thigh: That part of the hindquarter from the stifle to the hock, corresponding to the human shin and calf. Lower thigh.

Self color: One color or whole color except for lighter shadings.

Seeing Eye dog: A dog trained as a guide for the blind.

Semi-prick ears: Ears carried erect with just the tips leaning forward.

Septum: The line extending vertically between the nostrils.

Shelly: A shallow, narrow body, lacking the correct amount of bone.

Short back: A back shorter than the height at the withers, or one short in relation to specific breed requirements.

Shoulder-height: Height of dog's body as measured from the withers to the ground. *See* Withers.

Sickle hocked: Inability to straighten the hock joint on the back reach of the hind leg.

Sickle tail: Carried out and up in a semicircle.

Sire: The male parent.

Skully: Thick and coarse through skull.

Slab sided: Flat ribs with too little spring from spinal column.

Sled dogs: Dogs worked usually in teams to draw sleds.

Sloping shoulder: The shoulder blade set obliquely or "laid back."

Smooth coat: Short hair, close-lying.

Snipy: A pointed, weak muzzle.

Snow nose: Nose normally solid black, but acquires pink streak in winter. (Specified as acceptable in Siberian Husky standard.)

Soundness: The state of mental and physical health when all organs and faculties are complete and functioning normally, each in its rightful relation to the other.

Spay: To perform a surgical operation on the bitch's reproductive organs to prevent conception.

Spectacles: Shading or dark markings over or around the eyes or from eyes to ear.

Spike tail: Straight short tail that tapers rapidly along its length.

Splashed: Irregularly patched, color on white, or white on color.

Splayfoot: A flat foot with toes spreading. Open foot, open-toed.

Spread: Width between the forelegs when accentuated.

Spread hocks: Hocks pointing outward.

Spring of ribs: Curvature of ribs for heart and lung capacity.

Square body: A dog whose measurement from withers to the ground equals that from point of shoulder to the rearmost projection of the upper thigh.

Squirrel tail: Carried up and curving more or less forward.

Stance: Manner of standing.

Standard: A description of the ideal dog of each recognized breed, to serve as a word pattern by which dogs are judged at shows.

Standoff coat: A long or heavy coat that stands off from the body.

Staring coat: The hair dry, harsh, and sometimes curling at the tips.

Station: Comparative height from the ground, as high-stationed, low-stationed.

Steep: Used to denote insufficiently acute angles of articulation. For example, a steep front describes a more upright shoulder placement than is preferred.

Stern: Tail of a sporting dog or hound.

Sternum: Breastbone.

Stifle: The joint of the hind leg between the thigh and the second thigh. The dog's knee.

Stop: The step up from muzzle to skull; indentation between the eyes where the nasal bone and skull meet.

Straight-hocked: Lacking appreciable angulation at the hock joints. Straight behind.

Straight in pastern: Little or no bend between joint and foot.

Straight shoulders: The shoulder blades rather straight up and down, as opposed to sloping or "well laid back."

Stud book: A record of the breeding particulars of dogs of recognized breeds.

Stud dog: A male dog used for breeding purposes.

Substance: Bone.

Superciliary arches: The ridge, projection, or prominence of the frontal bone of the skull over the eye; the brow.

Swayback: Concave curvature of the back line between the withers and the hipbones.

Symmetry: Pleasing balance between all parts of the dog.

Tail set: How the base of the tail sets on the rump.

TD (Tracking Dog):   A suffix used with the name of a dog that has been recorded a Tracking Dog as a result of having passed an AKC licensed or member tracking test. The title may be combined with UDT title and shown as UDTX.

TDX (Tracking Dog Excellent):   A suffix used with the name of a dog that has been recorded a Tracking Dog Excellent as a result of having passed an AKC licensed or member tracking dog excellent test. The title may be combined with the UDT title and shown as UDTX.

Terrier: A group of dogs used originally for hunting vermin.

Terrier front: Straight front, as found on Fox Terriers.

Testicles: The male gonad; gland which produces spermatozoa. AKC regulations specify that a male that does not have two normal testicles normally located in the scrotum may not compete at any show and will be disqualified, except that a castrated male may be entered in Obedience Trials, Tracking Tests, Field Trials (except Beagles), and as Stud Dog in a Stud Dog class.

Thigh: The hindquarter from hip to stifle.

Throatiness: An excess of loose skin under the throat.

Thumb marks: Black spots on the region of the pastern.

Ticked: Small, isolated areas of black or colored hairs on a white ground.

Topknot: A tuft of longer hair on top of the head.

Topline: The dog's outline from just behind the withers to the tail set.

Toy dog: One of a group of dogs characterized by very small size.

Triangular eye: The eye set in surrounding tissue of triangular shape; three-cornered eye.

Tri-color: Three-color; white, black, and tan.

Trim: To groom the coat by plucking or clipping.

Triple Champion: A dog that has won bench show, field trial, and obedience trial championships.

Trot: A rhythmic two-beat diagonal gait in which the feet at diagonally opposite ends of the body strike the ground together; i.e., right hind with left front and left hind with right front.

Tuck-up: Characterized by markedly shallower body depth at the loin. Small-waisted.

Tulip ear: Ears carried with a slight forward curvature.

Turn-up: An uptilted foreface.

Type: The characteristic qualities distinguishing a breed; the embodiment of a standard's essentials.

UD (Utility Dog):   A suffix used with the name of a dog that has been recorded a Utility Dog by The AKC as a result of having won certain minimum scores in Utility Classes at a specified number of AKC licensed or member obedience trials. The title may be combined with TD or TDX title and shown as UDT or UDTX.

Underline: The combined contours of the brisket and the abdominal floor.

Undershot: The front teeth (incisors) of the lower jaw overlapping or projecting beyond the front teeth of the upper jaw when the mouth is closed.

Unsound: A dog incapable of performing the functions for which it was designed.

Upper arm: The humerus or bone of the foreleg, between the shoulder blade and the forearm.

Veil: The portion of the dog's forelock hanging straight down over the eyes, or partially covering them.

Vent: The anal opening.

Walk: Gaiting pattern in which three legs are in support of the body at all times, each foot lifting from the ground one at a time in regular sequence.

Walleye: An eye with a whitish iris; a blue eye, fisheye, pearl eye.

Webbed: Connected by a membrane. Webbed feet are important for water-retrieving breeds. (See Chesapeake Bay Retriever and Newfoundland standards.)

Weedy: An insufficient amount of bone; light-boned.

Well let down: Having short hocks.

Wet neck: Loose or superfluous skin; with dewlap.

Wheaten: Pale yellow or fawn color.

Wheel back: The back line arched markedly over the loin. Roached.

Whip tail: Carried out stiffly straight, and pointed.

Whisker: Longer hairs on muzzle sides and underjaw.

Winners: An award given at dog shows to the best dog (Winners Dog) and best bitch (Winners Bitch) competing in regular classes.

Wirehair: A coat of hard, crisp, wiry texture.

Withers: The highest point of the shoulders, immediately behind the neck.

Wrinkle: Loose, folding skin on forehead and foreface.

Wry mouth: Lower jaw does not line up with upper jaw.

Index

down/down-stay command, 88–89
dry (kibble) foods, 42–43
dual champion, 195

ears, breed selection, 8
Earthdog Tests, 102
Earthdog titles, 196
English Fox Hound, 141
English Springer Spaniel, 42
English Toy Spaniel, 53
estrus cycle, 111–112
Events Calendar, 182
exercise, 35, 66–67
eye contact, body language, 76
eyes, breed selection considerations, 8

feeding, 40–43
females (bitches)
    breeding, 112–113
    gestation period, 113–114
    reproductive physiology, 111–112
    spaying, 59–60
fencing, free-roaming dog deterrent, 63–65
Field Champion (FC) title, 102
Field Spaniel, 6, 183
Field Trial titles, 195
Field Trials, 102–104
Finnish Spitz, 115
first aid
    artificial respiration, 162–163
    bite wounds, 161
    bleeding, 162
    breathing problems, 162–163
    broken bones, 163
    heart massage, 163
    heart trouble, 163
    heatstroke, 163–164
    insecticides, 165
    moving injured dog, 160–161
    muzzle use, 159–160
    poisoning, 164–166
    rat poison, 165
    seizures/convulsions, 167
    shock, 167
    topical irritants, 168–169
foods
    bone cautions/concerns, 43
    table scraps, 41
    training philosophy, 77–78
    types, 42–43
Foundation Stock Service® (FSS), 13
functions (breed purpose), breed selection, 5–7,
    9–11

games, puppy play time, 34
German Shepherd Dog, 68
Giant Schnauzer, 5
Golden Retriever, 36, 44, 67
Gordon Setter, 47

grease, removing from coat, 168
Great Pyrenees, 16
Greater Swiss Mountain Dog, 49
grooming
    anal sac expressing, 54–55
    breed selection guidelines, 7–8
    brushes, 44–45
    combs, 45
    electric clippers, 49
    hair dryers, 46–47
    nail trimmers, 47–49
    puppies, 43–50
    scissors, 50
    shears, 50
    skunk odor removal, 52–53
    stripping implements, 46
    tables, 47
    teeth brushing, 53–54

hair dryers, 46–47
halters, training uses, 84
Handlers Program, 179
Harrier, 72
head collars/halters, training uses, 84
health
    breeding issues, 111
    neutering, 59–61
    puppy selection criteria, 26
    spaying, 59–61
    vaccinations, 56–58
health problems
    abscesses, 120
    allergies, 121–122
    anal irritation, 122
    arthritis, 123
    aural hematoma, 123
    balding, 123–124
    bladder infection, 124
    bladder stones, 124
    bloat, 124–125
    bronchitis, 125
    brucellosis, 126
    bumps, 145
    burns, 126
    cardiomyopathy, 126
    cataracts, 126
    cherry eye, 127
    chronic valvular disease, 127
    congenital heart disease, 140
    congestive heart failure, 140
    conjunctivitis, 129
    constipation, 129–130
    copraphagy (stool eating), 130
    corneal ulcer, 129
    cranial cruciate ligament injury, 130
    deafness, 131
    dental disease, 138–139

continued